Test-Driven Development in Swift

Compile Better Code
with XCTest and TDD

Gio Lodi

Apress®

Test-Driven Development in Swift: Compile Better Code with XCTest and TDD

Gio Lodi
Mount Martha, VIC, Australia

ISBN-13 (pbk): 978-1-4842-7001-1   ISBN-13 (electronic): 978-1-4842-7002-8
https://doi.org/10.1007/978-1-4842-7002-8

Copyright © 2021 by Gio Lodi

Managing Director, Apress Media LLC: Welmoed Spahr
Acquisitions Editor: Aaron Black
Development Editor: James Markham
Coordinating Editor: Jessica Vakili

Cover designed by eStudioCalamar

Cover image designed by Freepik (www.freepik.com)

Distributed to the book trade worldwide by Springer Science+Business Media New York, 1 NY Plaza, New York, NY 10014. Phone 1-800-SPRINGER, fax (201) 348-4505, e-mail orders-ny@springer-sbm.com, or visit www.springeronline.com. Apress Media, LLC is a California LLC and the sole member (owner) is Springer Science + Business Media Finance Inc (SSBM Finance Inc). SSBM Finance Inc is a **Delaware** corporation.

For information on translations, please e-mail booktranslations@springernature.com; for reprint, paperback, or audio rights, please e-mail bookpermissions@springernature.com.

Apress titles may be purchased in bulk for academic, corporate, or promotional use. eBook versions and licenses are also available for most titles. For more information, reference our Print and eBook Bulk Sales web page at http://www.apress.com/bulk-sales.

Any source code or other supplementary material referenced by the author in this book is available to readers on GitHub via the book's product page, located at www.apress.com/978-1-4842-7001-1. For more detailed information, please visit http://www.apress.com/source-code.

Printed on acid-free paper

*For Finn and Olive, who keep teaching me
how to be present and curious.*

*And for Nadine. It's not easy to put up with such a nerd,
but you do it anyway.*

Table of Contents

About the Author ....**xiii**

About the Technical Reviewer ....**xv**

Acknowledgments ....**xvii**

A Gift for You ....**xix**

Chapter 1: Why Test-Driven Development? **1**

What Is a Test? 1

Manual Testing Is Inefficient 2

Code That Checks Other Code 3

From Writing Tests to Writing Tests First...................................7

From Writing Tests First to Test-Driven Development 10

Key Takeaways 11

Endnote 12

Chapter 2: XCTest Introduction **13**

The Xcode Unit Test Target 13

XCTestCase and Equality Assertion 16

Other Assertions 18

Unwrapping Optionals 18

Expectations for Asynchronous Code 20

XCTestCase Life Cycle 22

Key Takeaways 25

Chapter 3: Getting Started with Test-Driven Development 27

Test List 28

Fake It…Till You Make It 29

Arrange, Act, Assert 32

First Make the Test Pass; then Make the Code Clean 34

The Compiler Is Part of the TDD Process 38

Wishful Coding 39

Key Takeaways 41

Chapter 4: Test-Driven Development in the Real World 43

The Menu Ordering App 43

Where to Begin? 44

Partition Problem and Solve Sequentially 45

Building the Menu 47

Use the Strictest Assertions Possible 52

Use the Clearest Assertion Possible 55

Don't Let the Tests Crash 56

Test Naming Conventions 60

Red, Green, and Don't Forget Refactor 62

Wiring Up the UI 63

Pure Functions 67

Key Takeaways 68

Chapter 5: Changing Tests with Fixtures 69

The Hidden Cost of Source Changes 70

Fixtures 71

Fixtures vs. Convenience Initializers 73

Fixtures Make the Test Actors Explicit 74

Fixtures Are Composable 76

Introduce Fixtures As Early As Possible 76

Practice Time 77

Key Takeaways..77

Endnote 78

Chapter 6: Testing Static SwiftUI Views 79

The Problem with Presentation Logic in the View......................................79

Decouple Presentation Logic from the View Implementation 81

Preparatory Refactor: Reduce the Working Surface Area 82

ViewModel 83

Using the ViewModel in the View 86

Beyond Testability 87

ViewModels Everywhere!..88

Key Takeaways...94

Endnotes 94

Chapter 7: Testing Dynamic SwiftUI Views...97

How SwiftUI and Combine Make Seamless View Updates Possible 98

Make the ViewModel Stream Updates with `ObservableObject`....................99

The Dependency Inversion Principle...105

Decouple the ViewModel from the Data Fetching with DIP 108

How to Test Async Updates of `@Published` Properties...............................111

Mystery Guest...115

Practice Time 116

Key Takeaways...117

Chapter 8: Testing Code Based on Indirect Inputs............................119

The Stub Test Double 120

Make Error Handling Explicit with `Result`....................................124

Practice Time 131

Key Takeaways... 132

Chapter 9: Testing JSON Decoding **133**

Option 1: Inline Strings... 137

Option 2: JSON Files.. 138

Which Option to Choose? 142

Is Testing JSON Decoding Worth It? 144

Practice Time 148

Key Takeaways... 149

Endnote 150

Chapter 10: Testing Network Code **151**

Why You Shouldn't Make Network Requests in Your Unit Tests 152

How to Decouple the Unit Tests from the Network 157

Simulate Network Requests Using a Stub 160

A Third-Party Alternative 163

Practice Time 164

Key Takeaways... 165

Endnote 166

Chapter 11: Injecting Dependencies with @EnvironmentObject **.....167**

How Dependency Injection Keeps Each Test Isolated 170

Dependency Injection vs. Directly Accessing Shared Instances.................. 176

Dependency Injection with @EnvironmentObject.................................... 177

The Downside of @EnvironmentObject 181

@EnvironmentObject vs. Directly Accessing Shared Instances 182

Practice Time 184

Key Takeaways... 184

Chapter 12: Testing Side Effects 185

Third-Party Dependencies Are the Same As All Dependencies.........................188

The Benefit of Abstracting Third-Party Dependencies 189

Build Wrappers for Third-Party Dependencies 189

The Spy Test Double..191

The Downside of Using Spies..194

Practice Time 195

Key Takeaways...195

Chapter 13: Testing a Conditional View Presentation.......................197

Informing the User of the Checkout Completion 198

How to Test Asynchronous Code When There Is No Callback.............................203

Wiring Up the View..208

Testing the Alert Dismiss Behavior...210

Key Takeaways...216

Chapter 14: Fixing Bugs and Changing Existing Code with TDD.......219

Fixing Bugs Driven by Tests 219

Changing Existing Code Driven by Tests 222

Key Takeaways...224

Chapter 15: Keeping Tests Isolated with Fakes and Clear with Dummies...225

Fake: How to Bypass Slow or Stateful Dependencies.....................................226

Dummy: How to Provide Dependencies That Are Required but Irrelevant
for the Behavior Being Tested 230

Key Takeaways...233

Chapter 16: Conclusion..**235**

More Than Just Testing...236

TDD and Software Design..237

TDD and Productivity..238

TDD and Product Development..239

Endnote..241

Cheatsheet..**243**

XCTest Test Structure...243

How to Test Asynchronous Code..244

How to Test Asynchronous Code When There Is No Callback..........244

How to Test Combine `Publishers`...245

How to Test Changes to SwiftUI `@Published` Properties.............247

Fixture Extension..248

Stub Test Double...248

Spy Test Double...249

Fake Test Double...249

Dummy Test Double...250

Appendix A: Where to Go from Here **251**

Continuous Integration..251

Snapshot Testing...252

UI Testing...253

API Integration Testing..254

Use Modularization to Tame Long Build Times........................255

How to Convince Your Team to Adopt TDD...............................256

Appendix B: Testing with Quick and Nimble..........................259

Nimble..260

Quick..262

Appendix C: TDD with UIKit.....................................267

How to Unit Test a `UIViewController`............................268

How to Test Table Views..273

How to Test ViewController Navigation and Presentation 276

What About AppKit and WatchKit?..................................281

Index..283

About the Author

Gio Lodi spent the past decade writing tests. He began with full-stack web development before moving into iOS programming and, more recently, into mobile infrastructure engineering. Ruby on Rails introduced him to the TDD (Test-Driven Development) world, and he fell in love with the fast-paced feedback loop: any hard problem could be decomposed in smaller and smaller parts until it got to an achievable size. When he first moved into the Apple ecosystem, Gio was surprised by the lack of comparable tools and started researching and experimenting with testing strategies and libraries, documenting his findings on his blog, and with talks and workshops at various industry conferences. He lives in an Australian beach town with his wife and two children and works remotely for Automattic, where he helps multiple teams shipping clean code that works on a schedule.

About the Technical Reviewer

Vishwesh Ravi Shrimali graduated in 2018 from BITS Pilani, where he studied mechanical engineering. Since then, he has worked with Big Vision LLC on deep learning and computer vision and was involved in creating official OpenCV AI courses. Currently, he is working at Mercedes-Benz Research and Development India Pvt. Ltd. He has a keen interest in programming and AI and has applied that interest in mechanical engineering projects. He has also written multiple blogs on OpenCV and deep learning on Learn OpenCV, a leading blog on computer vision. He has also coauthored *Machine Learning for OpenCV 4* (second edition) by Packt. When he is not writing blogs or working on projects, he likes to go on long walks or play his acoustic guitar.

Acknowledgments

This book wouldn't have been possible were it not for the giants whose shoulders I stood on. Tallest among all is Kent Beck, whose "rediscovery" of Test-Driven Development started the process, eventually bringing us here. Next to him are Michael Feathers, Martin Fowler, and Gary Bernhardt; their work instructed and inspired me.

Standing on giants' shoulders is a precarious predicament. Luckily, I had guardian angels that kept me from falling: my children motivated and helped me unplug; my wife patiently waited through all my "I just need five more minutes."

Many thanks to the team at Apress for taking a chance on me as a first-time author. In particular, thank you to Jessica Vakili: you've been patient and helpful. I owe a lot to Luca Ferrari and Mattia Toso. More than a decade ago, while attending Università degli Studi di Ferrara, they approached me to collaborate on a startup idea. We ended up using Ruby on Rails, which is how I stumbled upon Test-Driven Development. Also, thanks to Giulio Grillanda, Marco Bersani, and Matteo Bonora, who joined us and made the dream come true. You've all been incredible friends and supporters over the years – sorry for flying away and leaving you a pair of hands short.

Since 2014, I've been calling Melbourne, Australia, my home. Here, I've been lucky to find a friendly and welcoming community of like-minded folks with whom to share and sharpen ideas. Thanks to Aron Bury, Audrey Tam, Matt Delves, Pete Goldsmith, Stew Gleadow, and the Itty Bitty Apps crew for all the conversations and support and for being good friends. Special thanks to Adam Johnson, Charlie Scheer, Martin Heroux, and Richard Moult for the feedback on my early drafts and to Samuele

ACKNOWLEDGMENTS

Fiorini for the initial encouragement. I also want to thank Chris Toomey
and Steph Viccari, who keep sharing ideas on testing week after week on
The Bike Shed podcast, which is also where I heard the beautiful "helpful
pressure" analogy, and Ben Orenstein, from whom I learned about the
Mystery Guest pattern. Thank you to all those who deserve to be here, but
that, in my distraction, I forgot to mention.

Echoing Lynne Truss in *Eats, Shoots & Leaves*, I'd like to thank the
learned copy and technical editors who have attempted to sort out my
writing and save me from embarrassment. Where faults obstinately
remain, they are mine alone. Thank you to everyone who ever visited my
blog, `mokacoding.com`. Your feedback and support keeps fueling my work.

Finally, thank YOU, dear reader. Thank you for deciding to pick up this
book and share your valuable time with me.

A Gift for You

Thank you for reading this book. Your time is valuable; I consider it a privilege that you decided to spend it with me. As a sign of my gratitude, I want to offer something in return: for extra content, snippets, and further reading recommendations, head over to `https://tddinswift.com/gift` or just shoot me an email at hello@tddinswift.com.

If you enjoyed this book, please consider sharing it with a friend and leaving a review on your favorite platform. This goes a long way to help the book spread. I hope we can continue the conversation about how to write clean code that works. Don't hesitate to get in touch if you have any questions or to share your Test-Driven Development success story.

Thanks,

Gio

CHAPTER 1

Why Test-Driven Development?

What Is a Test?

The Oxford English Dictionary defines the noun *test* as: "*a procedure intended to establish the quality, performance, or reliability of something, especially before it is taken into widespread use.*"

In the context of software development, we can adapt the definition to: "*a procedure intended to establish the software quality, performance, or reliability, especially before it is shipped to the users.*"

To test our software essentially means to run it and verify it behaves as desired.

Take this "Hello, world!" script, for example:

```swift
#!/usr/bin/env xcrun swift

func main() {
    guard CommandLine.argc > 1 else {
        print("Hello, world!")
        return
    }
}
```

© Gio Lodi 2021

G. Lodi, *Test-Driven Development in Swift*, https://doi.org/10.1007/978-1-4842-7002-8_1

```
    print("Hello, \(CommandLine.arguments[1])!")
}

main()
```

A test for it could be to run it with no input, `./hello_world.swift`, and check that it prints "Hello, world!". We can then run it with a specific input and verify it uses it in the salutation. For example, `./hello_world.swift` Ada should print "Hello, Ada!".

In the same way, you can launch an iOS app in the Simulator and click through its UI to check it behaves as you programmed it to. Or you can submit data using a form in a web application and then check that the database contains it.

All the preceding examples share a trait: someone has to exercise the software and verify its behavior. They are *manual* tests.

To consistently ship quality software on a schedule, manual testing is not enough.

Manual Testing Is Inefficient

We can manually test a little script like `hello_world.swift` thoroughly because of its narrow feature set, but real-world programs are not as simple. Even in the smallest application, there are many possible code paths, many permutations of inputs the code accepts, and steps a user can take within the system. To test them all manually would take *a lot* of time.

Manual testing is costly as well as time consuming. Regardless of who performs the tests, whether it's software or QA engineers, product owners, or a third-party firm, real people have salaries to be paid. They also need time off to rest, get sick, may forget things, and, inevitably, make mistakes.

Skipping testing to save time and money would be a terrible move, though.

If we don't test our products before shipping them, the users will do it for us. That's far from ideal. While we might celebrate discovering a bug, a user would get frustrated and possibly leave our product for a competitor.

There must be a way to test our software to a high degree of confidence, fast, and without requiring humans to do all the work.

Code That Checks Other Code

Software developers write code to automate tasks that would otherwise be manual. Over the past decades, software has been "eating the world" as investor Marc Andreessen put it in a 2011 essay.

People used to send signed documents with a fax machine, carry big map books in their car, and store their business contacts in a Rolodex. Today, we have email with digital signatures, navigation apps leveraging the GPS in our smartphones, and CRM web tools.

Software can also automate other software, from identifying the best time for a meeting by reading the participants' calendars and generating invitations with a link to start a video call to publishing prewritten content on a schedule.

Verifying how software behaves is just another task ripe for automation. You can write code to check that the code you wrote behaves as expected.

Code that checks other code – that's what automated testing is.

To understand what writing code that checks other code means, let's turn to the programming interview all-time favorite: the "fizz-buzz" algorithm:

> Given an integer, print "fizz" if it's divisible by three, "buzz" if it's divisible by five, "fizz-buzz" if it's divisible by three and five; otherwise, print the value itself.

Here's one possible implementation:

```
func fizzBuzz(_ number: Int) -> String {
    let divisibleBy3 = number % 3 == 0
    let divisibleBy5 = number % 5 == 0

    switch (divisibleBy3, divisibleBy5) {
    case (false, false): return "\(number)"
    case (true, false): return "fizz"
    case (false, true): return "buzz"
    case (true, true): return "fizz-buzz"
    }
}
```

To test this code, we can use a script that calls fizzBuzz(_:) with different numbers and prints "PASSED" if the value is correct and "FAILED" if it isn't:

```
func testFizzBuzz() {
    if fizzBuzz(3) == "fizz" {
        print("PASSED")
    } else {
        print("FAILED")
    }

    if fizzBuzz(5) == "buzz" {
        print("PASSED")
    } else {
        print("FAILED")
    }

    // and so on
}
```

Repeating the if/else construct for each test would make the test long and boring to write. Let's extract the logic to check a value against an expected one in a dedicated function:

```
func test(value: String, matches expected: String) {
    if value == expected {
        print("PASSED")
    } else {
        print("FAILED")
    }
}

func testFizzBuzz() {
    test(value: fizzBuzz(1), matches: "1")
    test(value: fizzBuzz(3), matches: "fizz")
    test(value: fizzBuzz(5), matches: "buzz")
    test(value: fizzBuzz(15), matches: "fizz-buzz")
}
```

We now have an automated test script to verify our fizzBuzz(_:). If the output is all "PASSED," then the implementation is correct – or, to be more precise, matches the expectations we enumerated in the form of individual tests.

Automated testing outsources the need to type inputs, read outputs, and verify they are correct to a computer. Computers can do that faster and more accurately than any of us could.

Because of their speed, we can run automated tests more frequently, making it more likely to discover issues and catch regression early.

We can also automate the automated tests to never forget running them. For example, if you use Git, you could set up a hook that runs them before every commit.

Anyone can run all the tests because the script encodes them. Conversely, before someone can manually test a nontrivial product, they need training on it or won't know what to expect. Any new hire can run the test script and immediately tell whether all checks pass.

It might take longer to write an automated test for a behavior compared to manually testing it. Once you paid that one-time setup cost, though, you can run the test countless times in a fraction of what it would take to test manually.

Automated tests are by far the best investment you can make to maintain your software's quality as it evolves with new features and changes. They are a faster, cheaper, and scalable alternative to rote manual testing.

UNIT TESTS, INTEGRATION TESTS, UI TESTS... OH MY!

Reading material about software testing, you'll come across a variety of names for automated tests. Unit testing, integration testing, UI testing, property-based testing, exploratory testing, characterization testing, ... the list goes on. It's overwhelming, to say the least, and to make matters worse, different people or resources have different interpretations of what certain names actually mean.

Some scholars refer to any kind of automated test that doesn't involve interfacing with the actual UI of the app as a unit test; others adopt a stricter definition and consider unit tests only those tests that exercise a component in isolation. In this book, we'll follow Roy Osherove's definition of unit tests from *The Art of Unit Testing*:

> A unit test is a piece of code that invokes a unit of work and checks one specific end result of that unit of work.

where a unit of work is "the sum of actions that take place between the invocation of a public method in the system and a single noticeable end result by a test of that system."

Two other definitions worth giving are those of integration tests and UI tests.

Unit tests are the best tests to write when practicing Test-Driven Development because their sharp focus allows the faster feedback cycle to be possible. For that reason, this book focuses only on unit tests.

Every time we'll talk about "tests" in this book, it we'll be referring to unit tests, unless otherwise specified.

From Writing Tests to Writing Tests First

There is a problem with writing tests for code that already exists: you can't truly trust a test you haven't seen failing.

The only way to make sure your tests are not giving you a false positive – that they pass even though the code is wrong – is to modify the code's behavior to force a failure and see if they catch it.

Forcing failures in production code to verify the tests' correctness is not an efficient approach. It requires changing code you already wrote, only to undo the change right after, once you validated the test.

How can we verify that our tests are correct without going through the trouble of creating ad hoc failures?

The answer is by spinning the process around and writing the tests *first*.

By writing a test for something you haven't implemented yet, you can ensure the test will catch errors. That's because if there is not code for the behavior yet, the test *must* fail; if it doesn't, then it's not written correctly.

Let's look at the fizz-buzz example again. This time, we'll start with an empty implementation and then write one test for the expected behavior:

```
func fizzBuzz(_ number: Int) -> String {
    return ""
}
```

7

```
func testFizzBuzz() {
    test(value: fizzBuzz(1), matches: "1")
}
```

Running `testFizzBuzz()` will print "FAILED." To make the test pass, we need only to change the implementation to convert the input Int into a String:

```
func fizzBuzz(_ number: Int) -> String {
    return "\(number)"
}
```

If you now call `testFizzBuzz()`, it will print "PASSED."

Let's keep implementing `fizzBuzz(_:)` one test at a time and add a test to make sure an input divisible by three returns "fizz":

```
test(value: fizzBuzz(3), matches: "fizz")
```

To make both tests pass, we can update the `fizzBuzz(_:)` implementation to

```
guard number % 3 == 0 else { return "\(number)" }
return "fizz"
```

We can then continue with the next behavior facet – an input divisible by five should return "buzz":

```
test(value: fizzBuzz(5), matches: "buzz")
```

To make this new test and the other two pass, we can update `fizzBuzz(_:)` to

```
switch (number % 3 == 0, number % 5 == 0) {
case (true, false): return "fizz"
case (false, true): return "buzz"
default: return "\(number)"
}
```

We only have one scenario left to cover – numbers divisible by fifteen should return "fizz-buzz":

```
test(value: fizzBuzz(15), matches: "fizz-buzz")
```

Let's update fizzBuzz(_:) to make this final test pass too:

```
switch (number % 3 == 0, number % 5 == 0) {
case (false, false): return "\(number)"
case (true, false): return "fizz"
case (false, true): return "buzz"
case (true, true): return "fizz-buzz"
}
```

We got to a working "fizz-buzz" implementation by building it one step at a time, always starting from a failing test. Because each test represented a specific case of the overall "fizz-buzz" behavior, the code changed between iterations was always minimal. On each step, the test for the new behavior helped us verify if our new code worked without the need to call it manually multiple times, while the already existing tests ensured it didn't break the rest of the logic.

This test-first, step-by-step, fast-feedback way of writing code is incredibly effective. It's a unique way of building software called Test-Driven Development, TDD for short.

Test-Driven Development is the intentional and consistent use of the tests' feedback to inform the software implementation. But practicing TDD is more than just writing tests before production code; its by-products are far more valuable than the mere knowledge that your software behaves as expected.

From Writing Tests First to Test-Driven Development

Writing tests first puts helpful pressure on your software design. Environmental constraints and natural selection resulted in the evolution of the beautiful and advanced species that make up our world's flora and fauna. In the same way, forcing yourself to write tests first will push you and your codebase to a higher standard.

When you write tests first, you immediately see if your design is simple to test. Straightforward and isolated behavior is simpler to test than complicated one. A big object with many dependencies is harder to put in a test harness than a smaller one with only a few `init` parameters.

If code is straightforward to test, it will also be straightforward to work with it in production. That's because tests are consumers of the code's public API. Using code in the test is similar to using it in production.

Because writing simple tests is easier than writing complicated ones, you'll naturally gravitate toward code that is isolated and does only one thing. You'll build software made up of highly cohesive and loosely coupled components.

TDD also helps you have a better understanding of your products' requirements. To test your code's behavior, you need to know what it is first: you need to define inputs and their expected outputs concretely. To do so, you need to have appropriately assimilated the requirements for what the software should do. This upfront analysis makes implementing the code straightforward. Writing tests first removes the temptation to skip this critical step.

TDD gives you a psychological advantage. Developing your software one test at a time sets a sustainable pace, and our brains achieve goals better when the end is in sight.

Tackling the development of large complex applications one test at a time is the equivalent of how marathon runners approach their long races: putting one foot in front of the other.

Test-Driven Development is the keystone habit of software quality. When applied day after day, it has huge ripple effects on developer productivity, happiness, and software design quality.

As Kent Beck, the creator Test-Driven Development (or re-discoverer as he refers to himself[1]), puts it in *Test-Driven Development: By Example*:

> "If you're happy slamming some code together that more or less works and you're happy never looking at the result again, TDD is not for you. TDD rests on a charmingly naïve geekoid assumption that if you write better code, you'll be more successful. TDD helps you to pay attention to the right issues at the right time so you can make your designs cleaner, you can refine your designs as you learn."

In this book, you'll learn how to use TDD to build Swift applications, how the language strong type system augments your ability to write tests, and how to do so effectively using the Xcode IDE and XCTest framework provided by Apple. You'll see how this steady-paced, test-first approach can help you tackle problems of any size and complexity. You'll develop a feedback-first mindset, both for software and product development, to help you ship faster and learn more about what is valuable for your business.

Key Takeaways

- **Automated testing is the use of code to test other code**; it is cheaper, more effective, and far less error-prone than manual testing.

- **Writing tests first is better than doing so after the implementation is complete**; by seeing a test fail when there is no implementation for the behavior under test, you can trust it will catch future regressions.

- **Test-Driven Development is the practice of consistently and intentionally writing software starting from its tests**; this practice results in better software made up of highly cohesive and loosely coupled components, each responsible for a small and well-defined behavior.

Endnote

1. In Kent's own words: 'The original description of TDD was in an ancient book about programming. It said you take the input tape, manually type in the output tape you expect, then program until the actual output tape matches the expected output. After I'd written the first xUnit framework in Smalltalk I remembered reading this and tried it out. That was the origin of TDD for me. When describing TDD to older programmers, I often hear, "Of course. How else could you program?" Therefore I refer to my role as "rediscovering" TDD.' Source: `https://www.quora.com/Why-does-Kent-Beck-referto-the-rediscovery-of-test-driven-development-Whats-the-historyof-test-driven-development-before-Kent-Becks-rediscovery/answer/Kent-Beck`

CHAPTER 2

XCTest Introduction

In the previous chapter, we saw how to write code that tests code. While it was fun to construct a few functions to help us with that, to be productive and professional, it's much better to use a testing library.

A testing library, or framework in Swift terminology, provides the scaffold on which to build tests, run them, and gather their results. In the Apple ecosystem, XCTest is the default testing framework, and it comes bundled with the Xcode IDE.

If you like to get to know your tools before starting to work with them, you'll enjoy the following XCTest overview. If, on the other hand, you can't wait to write some *real* code, feel free to jump ahead to the next chapter and come back here later if you need.

There are other testing frameworks for Swift made by the open source community, but in this book we'll focus only on tests written in plain XCTest because it's the standard Apple technology and doesn't require any extra setup. The same Test-Driven Development applies, whether you use *vanilla* XCTest only or augment your setup with other testing libraries. Head over to Appendix B to learn about the open source frameworks Quick and Nimble.

The Xcode Unit Test Target

XCTest offers a test harness that integrates with Xcode making it easy to run tests and see their results in the IDE.

© Gio Lodi 2021
G. Lodi, *Test-Driven Development in Swift*, https://doi.org/10.1007/978-1-4842-7002-8_2

When you create a new project, Xcode lets you choose whether to add tests to it. If you choose so, Xcode will create two additional targets for you based on XCTest, one for unit tests and one for UI tests.

Figure 2-1 shows how to add tests when creating a new app.

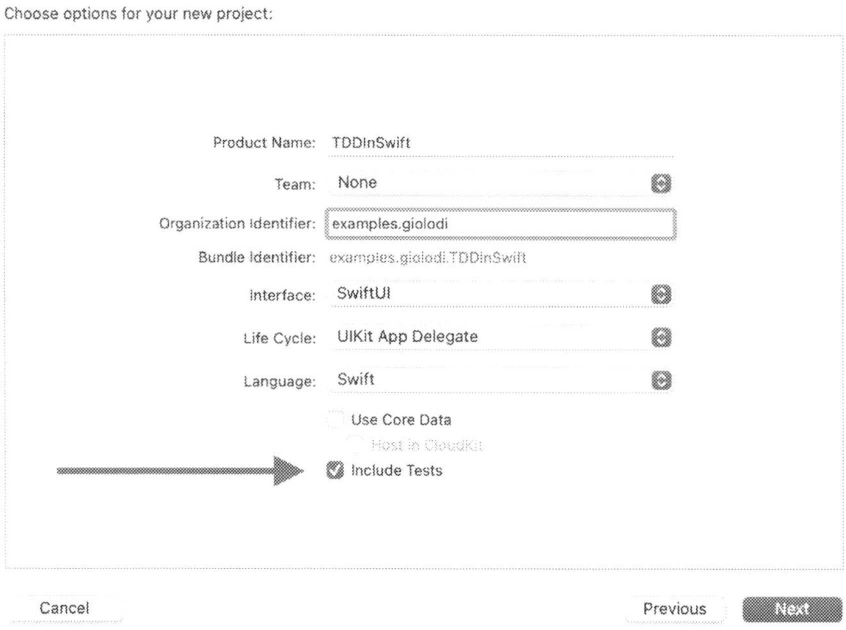

Figure 2-1. *The Xcode new application wizard, highlighting the option to add test targets to the project*

As we discussed in the previous chapter, unit and UI tests differ in that UI tests interact with the application as a black box, the same way a user would, while unit tests work on individual components. UI tests have their place, but you can't use them to drive the implementation of your software; to UI test a feature, you need to have written most of it already.

Conversely, tests in the unit test target run hosted in the application and have access to all the objects and types from its source code. This is exactly what we need to write tests first and use them as a fast-feedback mechanism on the correctness of the implementation.

In an Xcode unit test target, you are not limited to test where the object under inspection is isolated from the rest of the program; you can also write integration tests and any other kind of test where you may need to instantiate some of the objects in the source code directly, like snapshot or property-based testing.

If your app doesn't have a unit test target, you can add one from the project editor, selecting the button highlighted in Figure 2-2. This will bring up a wizard, see Figure 2-3, which lets you choose the type of target. If you filter for "test," you'll find the unit and UI test target options.

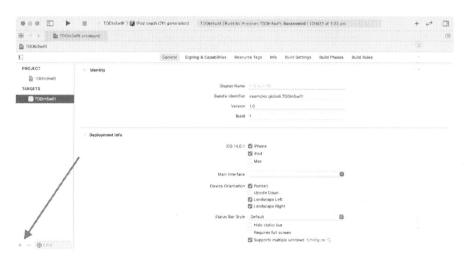

Figure 2-2. *The Xcode project editor, highlighting the button to add a new target*

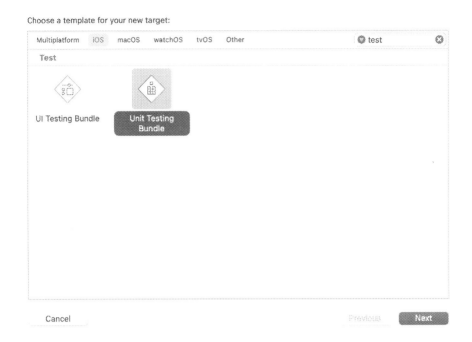

Figure 2-3. *The Xcode new target dialog, filtered for test targets only*

Now that we learned how to add the test target to our app, let's fill it up with tests by converting the bespoke tests we wrote in the previous chapter to XCTest.

XCTestCase and Equality Assertion

The starting point of every test is the XCTestCase class, which provides all the infrastructure and hooks to run tests and report their outcome. To create a new test, you make a subclass of XCTestCase, much like you would do with UIViewController:

```
import XCTest

class FizzBuzzTests: XCTestCase { }
```

XCTestCase is only the container for the tests, though. To define tests, you add an instance method to the class with a name starting with "test":

```
class FizzBuzzTests: XCTestCase {

    func testFizzBuzzDivisibleBy3ReturnsFizz() { }

    func testFizzBuzzDivisibleBy5ReturnsBuzz() { }

    func testFizzBuzzDivisibleBy15ReturnsFizzBuzz() { }

    func testFizzBuzzNotDivisibleBy3Or5ReturnsInput() { }
}
```

We can replace our custom function to check whether two Strings are equal with the XCTAssertEqual function:

```
func testFizzBuzzDivisibleBy3ReturnsFizz() {
    XCTAssertEqual(fizzBuzz(3), "fizz")
}
```

XCTAssertEqual works with types conforming to Equatable, so you can use it for many kinds of types, not only String.

If the values are not equal, the assertion will fail, and the framework will show a message:

```
func testFizzBuzzDivisibleBy3() {
    XCTAssertEqual(fizzBuzz(4), "fizz")
}
```

```
XCTAssertEqual failed: ("4") is not equal to ("fizz")
```

17

Other Assertions

You'll find yourself using XCTAssertEqual a lot, but that's not the only assertion the framework offers.

You can test Bool values:

XCTAssertTrue(true)
XCTAssertFalse(false)

You can test for nil values:

XCTAssertNil(nil)
XCTAssertNotNil("this is not nil")

There are assertions you can use to compare the values of types conforming to the Comparable protocol:

XCTAssertLessThan(1, 2)
XCTAssertGreaterThan(2, 1)
XCTAssertLessThanOrEqual(2, 2)
XCTAssertGreaterThanOrEqual(2, 1)

You can even test whether some code throws an error:

XCTAssertThrowsError(**try** aFunctionThatThrows())
XCTAssertNoThrow(**try** aFunctionThatThrows())

Unwrapping Optionals

Swift has a type called Optional to wrap those values that may or may not be nil.

Imagine you're writing a test for the getUserWithId(_:) method of a UserRepository object, which returns the User instance matching the given id if found or nil otherwise. The method return type is therefore Optional<User>, or the equivalent condensed version User?:

```
let user: User? = userRepository.getUserWithId(1)

XCTAssertEqual(user?.firstName, "John")
XCTAssertEqual(user?.lastName, "Appleseed")
```

Because the user is Optional, the preceding code accesses its properties using ?, the postfix optional chaining operator. If userRepository can't find a user for the id 1, the test will have two failures, one for each assertion.

XCTest has a special API to attempt unwrapping optional values and fail if they are nil, which we can use to improve that test:

```
let user: User = try XCTUnwrap(userRepository.getUserWithId(1))

XCTAssertEqual(user.firstName, "John")
XCTAssertEqual(user.lastName, "Appleseed")
```

Using XCTUnwrap, if getUserWithId returns nil, the test will fail at that point. This makes it clearer what the issues were, and so does having one failure instead of two. As a bonus, the syntax is cleaner without the ? postfix.

XCTUnwrap is also better than force-unwrapping optional values with !. If a test runs into a force-unwrapped Optional, which is nil, it will crash. When a test in the suite crashes, the whole suite stops so you only get information about the tests that run up to that point. On top of that, the error message for a crashed test is not as clear as a failed one, specially when run outside of Xcode. Preventing your test suite from crashing due to Optional values unexpectedly found nil will make it easier to triage test failures.

Expectations for Asynchronous Code

Testing asynchronous logic requires a few extra steps. Consider a function summing two `Ints` asynchronously and the result through a callback: `asyncSum(_ a: Int, _ b: Int, @escaping (Int) -> Void)`. If we wrote a test for `asyncSum` the same way we've been writing tests so far, it would fail:

```
var sum = 0

asyncSum(1, 2) { result in
    sum = result
}
```

```
XCTAssertEqual(sum, 3)
```

```
XCTAssertEqual failed: ("0") is not equal to ("3")
```

The reason for the failure is that, `asyncSum` being asynchronous, the callback assigning the summation result to `sum` runs *after* the assertion.

If you use a synchronous assertion to check the behavior of asynchronous code, the code might run before the assertion had a chance to execute, resulting, in the best case, in a false positive and, in the worst case, in a whole lot of time spent debugging tests with inconsistent behavior.

This is how to test asynchronous code in XCTest:

```
var sum = 0
let expectation = XCTestExpectation(description:
"Async sum completed.")
```

```
asyncSum(1, 2) { result in
    sum = result
    expectation.fulfill()
}
```

```
// This code waits for the `expectation` to be fulfilled (i.e.
// for its `fulfill()` method to have been called) for
// `timeout` seconds.
wait(for: [expectation], timeout: 0.2)

XCTAssertEqual(sum, 3)
```

Before running the asynchronous code, you instantiate an XCTExpectation, which will be fulfilled asynchronously. You can then tell your test to wait until the expectation has been fulfilled or a timeout has expired before continuing and only then run your assertions.

An even better way to write the preceding test is to perform the assertion right in the callback. This saves us the trouble of defining a variable to hold the value outside of the callback, making the test tidier:

```
let expectation = XCTestExpectation(description:
"Async sum completed.")

asyncSum(1, 2) { result in
    XCTAssertEqual(result, 3)
    expectation.fulfill()
}

wait(for: [expectation], timeout: 0.1)
```

Because we have the wait in the test, we are guaranteed the assertion will run, or the test will time out and fail.

A common case where you'll need to test asynchronous code is when working with the network, which we'll see in Chapter 10.

At WWDC 2021, Apple introduced a new alternative way to write asynchronous code using the async/await pattern available in Swift 5.5 for applications targeting iOS 15 or macOS 12. At the time of this writing, the implementation is still in beta and there is only a limited subset of applications that can will be able to adopt it once released because of the OS version requirements. Because of that, this book doesn't cover async/await.

XCTestCase Life Cycle

There is one last feature of XCTest that is worth knowing about when getting started, although it is one I strongly encourage you to avoid using unless you absolutely have to. XCTestCase offers methods to run code before each test or all the tests will run, as well as after each test or all the tests did run:

```swift
class LifeCycleExampleTest: XCTestCase {

    override class func setUp() {
        print("This runs before all tests")
    }

    override func setUpWithError() throws {
        print("This runs before each test")
    }

    override func tearDownWithError() throws {
        print("This runs after each test")
    }

    override class func tearDown() {
        print("This runs after all tests")
    }

    func testA() throws {
        print("This is test A")
    }
```

```
func testB() throws {
    print("This is test B")
}
}
```

This is the console output we'd get if we run `LifeCycleExampleTest`:

```
Test Suite 'LifeCycleExampleTest' started at ...
This runs before all tests
Test Case '-[Tests.LifeCycleExampleTest testA]' started.
This runs before each test
This is test A
This runs after each test
Test Case '-[Tests.LifeCycleExampleTest testA]' passed ...
Test Case '-[Tests.LifeCycleExampleTest testB]' started.
This runs before each test
This is test B
This runs after each test
Test Case '-[Tests.LifeCycleExampleTest testB]' passed ...
This runs after all tests
Test Suite 'LifeCycleExampleTest' passed at ...
    Executed 2 tests, with 0 failures (0 unexpected) in 0.003
    (0.003) seconds
```

As your code becomes more complicated, it might seem tempting to simplify your tests by preparing the components needed in the setUp methods or to clean up the state of the app after the tests run in the tearDown methods.

When your tests become complicated to set up, they are sending you a signal that the software design is getting complicated too. More often than not, using setUp and tearDown is the wrong answer to the problem of keeping tests tidy.

You're better off taking a step back and simplifying your design, perhaps by dividing an object with too many responsibilities into two or by injecting configurations rather than depending on the global state. I'll show you these and other techniques throughout the book.

There are two scenarios, though, in which I find `setUp` and `tearDown` useful. The first is when adding tests to code that depends on global state and doesn't have tests before making a change. Here, you should add your tests before making any change to the code, and so the life cycle methods are useful to start writing tests. Once you have your tests in place, you can refactor with confidence and remove the dependency on global state and the need to hook into the test life cycle.

The second case in which `setUp` and `tearDown` are the right tool for the job is in UI testing. We mentioned in the introduction that UI tests work with the app as a black box: you can't access individual components, and it's much harder to manipulate the global state of the application. `setUp` and `tearDown` are useful to prepare the app for the execution of certain UI tests and to clean up its state afterward.

XCTest has much more to offer, like skipping tests, defining execution context, or defining multiple test plans within Xcode to test the app in a permutation of different conditions. But that's enough theory for the moment.

Now that you've acquainted yourself with the tools, it's time to use them. In the next chapter, we'll see the basics of Test-Driven Development in Swift with XCTest.

Key Takeaways

- **XCTest is the framework Apple provides to write tests in Swift.**

- **Tests in XCTest are created with subclasses of XCTestCase, in functions with names starting with "test."**

- **XCTest offers several assertion functions to test code, like XCTAssertEqual, XCTAssertTrue, and XCTAssertFalse.**

- **Use XCTUnwrap to unwrap Optionals**; if the value is nil, the test will fail.

- **To test asynchronous code, define one or more XCTExpectations that the test will wait for and call their fulfill() method in the async logic.**

- **Test code that throws with XCTAssertThrows.**

- **Use setUpWithError and tearDownWithError to run logic before or after every test.** Use those methods sparingly; try to write tests that don't need extra setup or cleanup instead.

- **Use the class setUp and tearDown methods to run logic before or after all of the tests run.** Use these methods sparingly too.

CHAPTER 3

Getting Started with Test-Driven Development

In the previous chapters, we talked about the advantages of using tests to drive the design of the code and how to write tests using Apple's XCTest framework. It's now time to see concrete examples of Test-Driven Development.

We'll learn how to implement a piece of logic as an iterative process of writing tests and then making them pass. We'll see how TDD lets us focus first on getting the code right and then on making it clean. Finally, we'll discover how, in a language like Swift, the compiler complements the feedback loop that drives the software implementation and how to leverage it.

Test-Driven Development uses the feedback from the tests to guide the implementation of the production code.

How do you get this process going? How do you write Swift code starting from its tests with XCTest? The first step is understanding the behavior you need to implement.

© Gio Lodi 2021
G. Lodi, *Test-Driven Development in Swift*, https://doi.org/10.1007/978-1-4842-7002-8_3

Let's take this problem from exercism.io, a great place to hone your software skills:

> Write a function that, given an integer representing a year, tells whether the year is leap or not.
>
> A leap year in the Gregorian calendar occurs on every year that is evenly divisible by 4, except every year that is evenly divisible by 100, unless the year is also evenly divisible by 400.
>
> For example, 2021 is not a leap year, but 2020 is. 1900 is not a leap year, but 2000 is.

Here's a dummy version of the function, one that compiles but doesn't contain any of the necessary logic:

```swift
func isLeap(_ year: Int) -> Bool {
    return false
}
```

What sort of tests can we write to verify our code implements the behavior from the problem description?

Test List

The description itself already highlights the behavior details and even provides examples of inputs and outputs to verify:

- A year evenly divisible by 4 is leap, for example, 2020.

- A year evenly divisible by 100 is not leap, for example, 2100.

- A year evenly divisible by 400 is leap, for example, 2000.

- Any other year is not leap, for example, 2021.

We can write a test for each of those:

```
import XCTest

class LeapYearTests: XCTestCase {

    func testEvenlyDivisibleBy4IsLeap() {}

    func testEvenlyDivisibleBy100IsNotLeap() {}

    func testEvenlyDivisibleBy400IsLeap() {}

    func testNotEvenlyDivisibleBy4Or400IsNotLeap() {}
}
```

Notice I only wrote the test function's name, with no code inside. That's a *Test List*.

Writing a Test List is a way to start understanding the different details of what the code you're working on has to do.

The next step after defining the Test List is to write one and only one test. In TDD, we move in small, incremental steps, solving one problem at a time. That also applies to choosing which tests to write and how to write them. You want to get feedback as fast as possible. Writing one test is faster than writing all of them.

Fake It…Till You Make It

Which test should you begin with? A test you think you can make pass easily is a good choice. Starting with the most straightforward test is yet another technique to make the time to feedback as short as possible.

In this case, all the tests seem equally simple to me, so I'll start from the top:

```
func testEvenlyDivisibleBy4IsLeap() {
    XCTAssertTrue(isLeap(2020))
}
```

```
XCTAssertTrue failed
```

What's the easiest thing we can do to make this test pass? Just return the value that will make the test pass and work on the actual implementation later:

```
func isLeap(_ year: Int) -> Bool {
    return true
}
```

This technique of returning a hardcoded value that will make the test pass is called "Fake It". Fake It makes it easy to get started writing code when you are unsure about the implementation details. Use a fake implementation so you can get some tests running first and learn from them.

For leapYear, where the implementation is straightforward, Fake It might be overkill. If an obvious implementation to make a test pass comes to mind, feel free to write it without faking it first. You'd be surprised, though, how many times Fake It can be just what you need to get unblocked and start solving the problem.

Thanks to the fake implementation, our test is now green. What's the next step?

Now that we established a baseline with the green test, we could work on the actual implementation, confident that the code is correct if the test stays green. On the other hand, we still have more tests to write, so in this case, I'd move on to the next test instead.

A good next test to write is the one for an input that is not divisible by 4, the opposite of the test we just wrote:

```
func testNotEvenlyDivisibleBy4Or400IsNotLeap() {
    XCTAssertFalse(isLeap(2021))
}
```

```
XCTAssertFalse failed
```

We're already at the point where we can't fake the implementation anymore. Using another hardcoded value wouldn't make both tests pass:

```
func isLeap(_ year: Int) -> Bool {
    return year % 4 == 0
}
```

Let's move to the next test:

```
func testEvenlyDivisibleBy100IsNotLeap() {
    XCTAssertFalse(isLeap(2100))
}
```

```
XCTAssertFalse failed
```

The simplest thing I can think of to make it pass is to add a guard statement:

```
func isLeap(_ year: Int) -> Bool {
    guard year % 100 != 0 else { return false }
    return year % 4 == 0
}
```

We only have one more test to write:

```
func testEvenlyDivisibleBy400IsLeap() {
    XCTAssertTrue(isLeap(2000))
}
```

```
XCTAssertTrue failed
```

Like in the preceding, the simplest thing I can think of is a guard:

```swift
func isLeap(_ year: Int) -> Bool {
    guard year % 400 != 0 else { return true }
    guard year % 100 != 0 else { return false }
    return year % 4 == 0
}
```

All our tests are passing. We have a complete function to evaluate whether a given year is leap.

We got here by writing one test, watching it fail, using the failure message to write just enough code to make the test pass, and then repeating the process for the next test. Red, green, red, green, red, green.

We didn't set ourselves the lofty goal of writing a working implementation in one go. Instead, we used the feedback from the tests to build it one little bit at a time, writing the simplest code we possibly could.

Often, the simplest code you'll write to make the tests pass is quite ugly. That's okay. Remember: small incremental steps. First, make the code work, and then make it clean.

Having the tests and knowing they cover code's behavior because you've seen them all go from red to green gives you the confidence to refactor. To refactor means to change how the code looks without affecting its behavior. Refactoring is a core part of TDD.

Before looking at how refactoring fits into the workflow, let me say a word on the test's structure.

Arrange, Act, Assert

The tests we used to drive the leap year implementation were all one-liners. The subject under test, its input and output, and the assertion on the expected behavior all fit nicely in a single line:

```
func testEvenlyDivisibleBy4IsLeap() {
    XCTAssertTrue(isLeap(2020))
}
```

When the behavior under test is not as trivial as a method taking one input and returning a `Bool`, it's useful to structure the test by explicitly separating it into three stages:

- **Arrange**: Prepare the inputs.

- **Act**: Exercise the behavior under test.

- **Assert**: Verify the output matches the expectation.

Let's rewrite the preceding test following "Arrange, Act, Assert":

```
func testEvenlyDivisibleBy4IsLeap() {
    let year = 2020            // Arrange

    let leap = isLeap(year) // Act

    XCTAssertTrue(leap)        // Assert
}
```

Organizing your tests clearly and consistently will help you navigate them because they will all present the same structure. Finding the inputs, the method under test, or the assertions will be easier because they'll always be in the same location relative to the test. The proverb "a place for everything and everything in its place" applies to your codebase as well as your house.

Another formulation of the three stages is "Given, When, Then." Given a year evenly divisible by 4, when calling `isLeap(_:)`, then the result is `true`.

"Given, When, Then" is more suited for higher-level tests, such as UI tests looking at full user journeys: given an authenticated user, when loading the setting screen, then the authentication prompt is presented. Because this book focuses on unit tests, we'll use "Arrange, Act, Assert".

Now that we've learned how to structure our tests, let's see how refactoring fits into the Test-Driven Development process.

First Make the Test Pass; then Make the Code Clean

Test-Driven Development frees you from the mental burden of having to write code that is at the same time working and clean. First, the tests guide you in writing code that works. Then, they give you the confidence to focus on making it clean.

Imagine you have a `Product` value type defined like this:

```
struct Product {
    let category: String
    let price: Double
}
```

You need to write a function that, given an array of sold `Products` and a category value, returns the total amount sold for that category:

```
func sumOf(_ products: [Product], withCategory category: String) -> Double {
    return 0.0
}
```

Let's start with the Test List:

```
import XCTest

class SumOfProductsTests: XCTestCase {

    func testSumOfEmptyArrayIsZero() {}
```

```
func testSumOfOneItemIsItemPrice() {}

func testSumIsSumOfItemsPricesForGivenCategory() {}
}
```

Let's start with the first test: the product category sum of an empty array should be zero. Behavioral *edges* like this one are usually simpler to implement. In this case, because the input array is empty, we know the implementation will involve very little logic, which gives us a chance to lay the functional scaffold on which we'll then build the complete behavior:

```
func testSumOfEmptyArrayIsZero() {
    let category = "books"
    let products = [Product]()

    let sum = sumOf(products, withCategory: category)

    XCTAssertEqual(sum, 0 )
}
```

Because the dummy implementation of the function returns 0, the test passes already. That's okay with me. I know that as we'll add more tests, they'll require the implementation to be correct.

Let's keep building up to our complete implementation by tackling the other behavioral edge case:

```
func testSumOfOneItemIsItemPrice {
    let category = "books"
    let products = [Product(category: category, price: 3)]

    let sum = sumOf(products, withCategory: category)

    XCTAssertEqual(sum, 3)
}
```

```
XCTAssertEqual failed: ("0.0") is not equal to ("3.0")
```

Here's the first implementation that I came up with:

```
var sum = 0.0
for product in products {
    sum += product.price
}
return sum
```

The tests are now passing. It's time to ask the question: is there a better way to write this code?

I prefer collection manipulations over for loops. How does this look?

```
return products.reduce(0.0) { $0 + $1.price }
```

The tests still pass, and we got rid of the need to define a var to collect the sum as we iterate through the array.

The tests helped us make sure that our change in the code's implementation didn't affect its behavior. That's the definition of a refactor: a change in the way the code is written that doesn't change its behavior.

There's only one test left to write, the one for the function's main use case:

```
func testSumIsSumOfItemsPricesForGivenCategory() {
    let category = "books"
    let products = [
        Product(category: category, price: 3),
        Product(category: "movies", price: 2),
        Product(category: category, price: 1)
    ]

    let sum = sumOf(products, withCategory: category)

    XCTAssertEqual(sum, 4)
}

XCTAssertEqual failed: ("6.0") is not equal to ("4.0")
```

This test doesn't pass because there is no logic to select only the Products matching the given category:

```
return products.reduce(0.0) {
    guard $1.category == category else { return $0 }
    return $0 + $1.price
}
```

With this updated implementation, the test passes; therefore, the implementation works. Again, let's ask the question: can we improve it?

I like how the code steps through the array only once, but I'd rather have the filtering operation separate from the summation:

```
return products
    .filter { $0.category == category }
    .reduce(0.0) { $0 + $1.price }
```

I think this reads better; it clearly says "given some products, take the ones matching a category and then sum their price."

Once again, we moved from the red state to the green one and then refactored the code.

Red, green, refactor. That's the TDD mantra.

Forcing yourself to write code that works, is elegant, and has no duplication requires more energy than solving each of those problems in isolation. Test-Driven Development gives you the process to fully focus on one problem at a time.

That's not to say you should intentionally write dirty or suboptimal code just to make the tests pass if you already have a better solution in mind. Write the first implementation that comes to you, then, once you made the tests green, ask yourself whether you can improve the code. You'll be surprised and delighted at how many times you'll answer yes.

We've seen how a failing test acts as a feedback mechanism on the code's correctness and as a suggestion on what to implement next. In Swift, we can leverage another feedback mechanism as powerful as the failing tests: the compiler.

The Compiler Is Part of the TDD Process

The introduction of Swift in 2014 was a big revolution in the Apple development ecosystem. With its strong type system, it was a change of course from Objective-C's dynamic nature.

A strong type system removes a whole set of type mismatch runtime errors. If you modify a function to return `Array<String>` instead of `String`, all its callers will fail to compile with "Cannot convert value of type '`Array<String>`' to specified type '`String`'." In a dynamic language, the app would have still run, only to fail as soon as it tried to call a `String` method on the returned array value.

Strong types also help you make inconsistent state *impossible to represent*. My favorite example is using an `enum` to represent the mutually exclusive states as opposed to a set of nullable properties for each possible value:

```
let responseValue: Value?
let responseError: Error?

// vs

let response: Result<Value, Error>
```

With the `responseValue` and `responseError` pair, you need to write a test to ensure that if one is `nil`, the other has a value and that they're never `nil` at the same time. Using the `Result` enum shifts this test to the type system level. The compiler enforces the mutually exclusive relationship; you don't need to write a test for it.

When you look at the code through the lens of the tests, having a strong type system makes a whole set of tests unnecessary.

In a strongly typed language, TDD is as much Test-Driven Development as it is *Type-Driven* Development. Compiler errors are like test failures: they give you feedback on your code's correctness, and you can encode tests in your objects and functions type signatures.

Let's see how we can leverage the compiler to know what code to write next the same way we do when reading test failures.

Wishful Coding

In the leapYear exercise, we started with a dummy function implementation before writing the tests. A different approach is to write the function only when there is a compiler error telling us it's needed:

```
import XCTest

class LeapYearTests: XCTestCase {
    func testEvenlyDivisibleBy4IsLeap() {
        XCTAssertTrue(isLeap(4))
        // Compiler says: Cannot find 'isLeap' in scope
    }
}
```

The compiler can't find a function with a signature matching the one we wrote. We are in the red state, only we don't have a test failure but a compiler one. Like test failures, compiler errors are suggestions on what to do next to get to the green state. If the compiler can't find a function called isLeap, let's define one for it:

```
func isLeap(_ year: Int) {}
```

The compiler has a new error now:

```
XCTAssertTrue(isLeap(4)) // Compiler says: Cannot convert value
                         // of type '()' to expected argument
                         // type 'Bool`
```

XCTAssertTrue expects a Bool to check, but our isLeap function is not returning anything right now, or rather, it returns (), which means Void:

```
func isLeap(_ year: Int) -> Bool {
    return true
}
```

Now the code compiles, and we can run the tests to see if the implementation works.

What we did here was writing the code we wished we had before defining it and then using the compiler errors as a guide on how to get to the function definition. This technique is called Wishful Coding.

Wishful Coding may seem like an overly long process, especially for straightforward code like the leapYear function. Am I advocating you should *always* use this approach? No, but I want you to be aware of this technique.

Next time you feel stuck coming up with a function signature up front, write the code you wish you had in the test assertion, then see how the compilation fails, and start by addressing that error.

I encourage you to try this, even if you feel like you might be going a bit slower. In the boxing movie *Rocky III*, Apollo Creed brings a sad and defeated Rocky to the swimming pool to "strengthen and use muscles he never thought he had." Rocky is awkward and slow at first but eventually swims laps upon laps – accompanied by an inspiring soundtrack – and goes off to reclaim his title.

Techniques like Wishful Coding and Fake It are like muscles you didn't know you had. You need to exercise and strengthen them so that when the time will come to use them, they'll be ready to spring into action.

Now that we've seen what the staples of Test-Driven Development are, it's time to apply them in the real world. In the next chapter, well start the Test-Driven Development of a new application.

Key Takeaways

- **Test List**: Start listing all the tests you might need to verify the behavior of the code you need to implement.

- **Red, green, refactor**. Tackling one test at a time, write the test, watch it fail because there is no implementation for that behavior, and then use the failure as a guide on what to do to make the test pass. Once the test passes, ask yourself whether the code can be improved.

- **TDD lets you focus on making the code work first and then making it clean**. Tackling each task in isolation is easier than trying to do both at the same time. The tests give you the confidence to iterate on your implementation.

- **Structure your tests in three stages: Arrange, Act, Assert**. Clearly and consistently separating the inputs, the behavior under test, and the expectation on its output will reduce the cognitive load of reading tests.

- **Compiler errors are a source of feedback too**.

41

- **Fake It**. If you are not sure how to implement something, start by hardcoding the value that will make the test pass. Once you have a green test, you can work on the real implementation with confidence.

- **Wishful Coding**: If you are not sure how to define a function or type, start by writing its usage in the test and use the compiler's failure message as the starting point for the definition.

CHAPTER 4

Test-Driven Development in the Real World

How do you go from using tests to drive the implementation of small, self-contained problems like the ones we've seen in the previous chapters to building a full application?

By cheating. Instead of seeing the application as a whole problem, you can break it apart into smaller and smaller ones. Eventually, you'll reach a scale where each problem is small and self-contained.

In this chapter, we'll start building the real-world application that we'll use as our playground throughout the book. We'll apply the *Partition Problem and Solve Sequentially* technique to identify the initial feature set and decide which to begin with. We'll then use tests to drive the first kernel of functionality, learning why you should use the strictest assertions possible and why you shouldn't let your tests crash.

The Menu Ordering App

Alberto, the owner of your local Italian restaurant, hired you to build his new ordering app.

© Gio Lodi 2021
G. Lodi, *Test-Driven Development in Swift*, https://doi.org/10.1007/978-1-4842-7002-8_4

The first thing you did together was defining the minimum viable feature set. In version 1.0, customers will be able to browse the menu, select dishes, and submit and pay their orders.

This initial version is minimal and streamlined, but there are nevertheless a number of questions to answer. Here are some, and more will likely arise as you progress in the development:

- Where does the data for the menu come from?

- How do patrons build up their order?

- How do they pay?

- How is the order sent to the kitchen

- What happens if there is an error?

The good news is you don't need to answer them all right now!

Trying to answer every design question up front can impede the effectiveness of your architecture. Addressing each decision individually as the software implementation demands an answer gives you time to better understand the requirements and discover the project's nuances. As you keep developing the app, you gain more context and experience on the problem you're trying to solve. That puts you in a better position to make an optimal design decision.

If writing the code helps generate the understanding that will inform the application's design, which code should you begin to write?

Where to Begin?

There are a few options for where to begin building your app. One is to start with the hardest thing, the task where you have the most learning to do. Unknowns are where most of the project risk is, so it's helpful to tackle them up front to avoid nasty surprises later down the track.

You could also start from the easiest thing – that is, something you already know how to do. Here the advantage is that you get the ball rolling quickly and build momentum in your development process.

Yet another option is to begin with something that makes later work possible. In our app, displaying the menu sits nicely in between being a straightforward task with few moving parts and being a precondition for other features; without the menu, customers can't make an order.

Starting with displaying the menu also has the advantage of giving us something to share with Alberto early on: an incomplete but functioning version of the app to show our progress.

Partition Problem and Solve Sequentially

Practicing Test-Driven Development is an exercise in decomposition and sequentiality. You take a requirement for a method and partition it into a list of tests to work sequentially. For each test, you split making the test pass from cleaning the implementation. You write as little code as necessary to get to the green state first and then move on refining the production code.

I call this approach *Partition Problem and Solve Sequentially*. This strategy is fractal; we can apply it again and again, from the macro-level of the app architecture as a whole to the micro-level of a single test. What is the list of design decisions in the previous section if not a partitioned view of the higher-level task of building the app?

Let's apply Partition Problem and Solve Sequentially to the starting point of the app, displaying the menu. Let's break it down into core questions to answer:

- How does the UI look like?

- Where does the data come from?

- How is the data organized in the UI?

We don't need to give these questions a final answer. We are interested in building something as fast as possible to learn from the process.

How does the UI look like? Stock UI will do for now; we can work on the look and feel once we laid out a solid functionality core.

Where does the data come from? A remote API, so it's always up to date? A file bundled in the app? We don't need to decide where the data comes from to display it: a hardcoded list will do for now.

How is the data organized? Let's start by copying what the physical menu does. Items are grouped into categories: starters, pastas, drinks, and desserts.

By sidestepping the UI and data source questions, we can focus entirely on the core task of implementing the data organization for the app.

Don't confuse the act of delaying giving a final answer to those questions with laziness. By simplifying the problem, we set ourselves an achievable goal on which we can make concrete progress. We'll have something we can share with our client as early as possible.

Henrik Kniberg refers to this approach as Earliest Testable/Usable/Lovable. Suppose our task is to build an efficient means of transportation for our users. We're better off starting with a skateboard and iterating our way up to an electric car, rather than building the wheels first, then the frame, and so on. We can deliver a skateboard sooner than a car. People can move around using skateboards; a car wheel by itself won't get them anywhere.

Also, notice that these simplifications don't constrain the system; they make it more flexible. By waiting to decide where the data comes from, we have kept the door open for any option.

Through this decomposition process, we now have a spec for our Earliest Testable version: an app that displays a hardcoded menu in a stock list view, grouped by category. Let's get coding.

Building the Menu

Let's say our menu data is a flat array of dishes. To display it sorted by category, we need a function that, given an array of dishes, returns an array of sections, where each section holds all the items of a single category.

Are there edge cases in the behavior?

- If all the dishes in the array are of the same category, we should have only one section.

- If the input array is empty, the output sections array should be empty too.

Let's create a new file in the test target and translate these requirements into a Test List:

```
// MenuGroupingTests.swift
@testable import Albertos
import XCTest

class MenuGroupingTests: XCTestCase {

    func testMenuWithManyCategoriesReturnsOneSectionPer
    Category() {}

    func testMenuWithOneCategoryReturnsOneSection() {}

    func testEmptyMenuReturnsEmptySections() {}
}
```

Which test should we begin with? As we've seen in the previous chapter, a test we are confident we can make pass is a good place to start. The behavioral edges are usually simpler; the test for "empty input produces empty output" should be straightforward.

Working from the edges inward will also give us a chance to focus on building the function scaffold first and then laying the individual bricks that make up the complete behavior on top of it one at a time.

Where should we start writing the test? From the assertion that will pass once the behavior is implemented. In this test, we want to assert that the sections array is empty:

```
func testEmptyMenuReturnsEmptySections() {
    // Arrange the input: an empty menu

    // Act on the SUT to get the output: the sections array

    XCTAssertTrue(sections.isEmpty)
}
```

Where does `sections` come from? It's the return value of the function we are trying to write:

```
func testEmptyMenuReturnsEmptySections() {
    // Arrange the input: an empty menu

    let sections = ???

    XCTAssertTrue(sections.isEmpty)
}
```

How does the function returning `sections` look like? It should be something taking an empty array as input, and its role is to group a flat menu by category:

```
func testEmptyMenuReturnsEmptySections() {
    let menu = [MenuItem]()

    let sections = groupMenuByCategory(menu)

    XCTAssertTrue(sections.isEmpty)
}
```

At this point our test is ready, but it doesn't compile:

```
let sections = groupMenuByCategory(menu)
// Compiler says:
// Cannot find `groupMenuByCategory` in scope
```

The compiler error gives us a hint on what to do next: we need to define groupMenuByCategory():

```
func groupMenuByCategory(_ menu: [MenuItem]) -> [MenuSection] {
    return []
}
```

As part of defining the function, we also wrote names for the types it works with, but since we haven't defined them yet, the code still doesn't compile.

I'm using the *Wishful Coding* technique introduced in Chapter 3 to better show the full test-driven flow step-by-step.

As you become more confident with TDD, you'll be able to write empty function and type definitions before the tests and leverage Xcode's autocompletion for a slightly faster process.

The compiler says:

- Cannot find type MenuItem in scope
- Cannot find type MenuSection in scope

Let's define these types in dedicated files in the application target:

```
// MenuItem.swift
struct MenuItem {}
```

```
// MenuSection.swift
struct MenuSection {}
```

The code now compiles. If you run the tests with the Cmd U keyboard shortcut, you'll see they pass.

Why didn't we add any properties to MenuItem or MenuSection? We'll need properties in those types for them to be useful, of course, but we should wait to add them till a test that shows we need them. TDD pushes you to move in small steps, get feedback as fast as possible, and only write as little code as you need.

Writing just enough code is also an excellent guardrail against overengineering. Because we write the tests before the production code and we only write tests for the behavior we need in the app right now, the resulting production code is precisely the one we need, nothing more, nothing less.

Continuing to work from the edge cases inward, the next test to tackle is the one for an input with items all from the same category:

```
func testMenuWithOneCategoryReturnsOneSection() {
    let menu = [???]
    let sections = groupMenuByCategory(menu)

    XCTAssertEqual(sections.count, 1)
}
```

How can we build an input array of menu items all of the same category? In the test, we can write

```
let menu = [
    MenuItem(category: "pastas"),
    MenuItem(category: "pastas")
]
```

This code doesn't compile:

```
let menu = [
    MenuItem(category: "pastas"),
        // Compiler says: Argument passed to call
        // that takes no arguments
    MenuItem(category: "pastas")
        // Compiler says: Argument passed to call
        // that takes no arguments
]
```

Because our MenuItem has no properties, its compiler-generated initializer takes no arguments. We can make the code build by defining the property we need:

```
struct MenuItem {
    let category: String
}
```

The test now compiles but is still red. It's time to take our first stab at returning an array of MenuSections.

The only requirement of this test is that the return value has one element. We can simply create the array of MenuSections using all of the input MenuItems and think about the grouping by category when a test will require us to do so:

```
func groupMenuByCategory(_ menu: [MenuItem]) -> [MenuSection] {
    guard menu.isEmpty == false else { return [] }

    return [MenuSection()]
}
```

Both our tests pass, but you might have noticed something odd in the current behavior: given an input array of MenuItems, all from the same category, we are getting an array with a single MenuSection, but that section has no information because the type has no properties. The only thing we know from the return value is that the input had more than zero items.

Our goal as we move from one test to the next is to progress through *working* implementations. Right now, we're falling short. The reason I got us to this point is that I used an assertion that wasn't thorough enough.

Use the Strictest Assertions Possible

A useful thought experiment to do when reviewing unit tests is to think whether you could write code that is wrong but still makes the test pass. If you can, then there is a hole in the test net.

That's precisely the state we are in right now: the code is correct from the test's point of view but doesn't implement the desired behavior – however incomplete that might be at this stage.

How can we make our test more thorough? What properties should the correct [MenuSection] output have, given the [MenuItem] input we provided?

The returned MenuSection should hold all the elements from the [MenuItem] input. As we've just seen, simply counting the elements in an array is not enough; we also need a way to compare the MenuItems in the section to ensure they are all in the output.

We need to add an items: [MenuItem] property to MenuSection and a name: String property to MenuItem. We knew we'd need these properties from the start, but we're adding them only now because we finally have a test that can exercise them.

As usual, the first step is to write the code we wish we had in the test:

```
func testMenuWithOneCategoryReturnsOneSection throws {
    let menu = [
      MenuItem(category: "pastas", name: "name"),
                // Compiler says: Extra argument
                // 'name' in call
      MenuItem(category: "pastas", name: "other name"),
                // Compiler says: Extra argument
                // 'name' in call
    ]

    let sections = groupMenuByCategory(menu)

    XCTAssertEqual(sections.count, 1)
    let section = try XCTUnwrap(sections.first)
    XCTAssertEqual(section.items.count, 2)
                // Compiler says: Value of type 'MenuSection'
                // has no member 'items'
    XCTAssertEqual(section.items.first, "name")
                // Compiler says: Value of type 'MenuSection'
                // has no member 'items'
    XCTAssertEqual(section.items.last, "other name")
                // Compiler says: Value of type 'MenuSection'
                // has no member 'items'
}
```

Before tackling the compiler errors, let's have a look at the assertions in the tests.

After checking that sections contains only one element, we use XCTUnwrap to get a nonoptional reference to it and avoid having to access its elements with the ? postfix optional chaining operator. See Chapter 2 for more information on XCTUnwrap.

Next, we check that `section.items` has two elements, that is, the section has all the elements in the input.

We could have stopped here, but to be sure that as well as having *all* the MenuItems for the category the result has *only* the menu items we also make, check that the items in the section are the same as the input by comparing their names.

To have a tight check, we need both assertions. Checking the names makes sure the section contains all input MenuItems; checking the count makes sure it contains *only* the input MenuItems for the given category.

The compiler errors are all because the value types don't have those new properties in their definitions:

```swift
// MenuItem.swift
struct MenuItem {
    let category: String
    let name: String
}

// MenuSection.swift
struct MenuSection {
    let items: [MenuItem]
}
```

After this change, we have a new compiler error:

```swift
func groupMenuByCategory(_ menu: [MenuItem]) -> [MenuSection] {
    guard menu.isEmpty == false else { return [] }
    return [MenuSection()]
    // Compiler says:
    // Missing argument for parameter 'items' in call
}
```

Because we updated the definition of MenuSection, the compiler-generated init changed too. The simplest thing to do to make the tests compile is to return an empty array:

```
return [MenuSection(items: [])]
```

Now our tests fail with

```
XCTAssertEqual(section.items.count, 2)
    // XCTAssertEqual failed:
    // ("0") is not equal to ("2")
XCTAssertEqual(section.items.first?.name, "name")
    // XCTAssertEqual failed:
    // ("nil") is not equal to ("Optional("name")")
XCTAssertEqual(section.items.last?.name, "other name")
    // XCTAssertEqual failed:
    // ("nil") is not equal to ("Optional("other name")")
```

To complete this slice of behavior, simply use the input menu as the items value:

```
return [MenuSection(items: menu)]
```

Now we're back in the green state; the behavior is incomplete, but we know it's correct.

The thoroughness of the assertions affects a test's accuracy, so remember to dig as deep as possible with the checks you make.

Use the Clearest Assertion Possible

Another thing to notice when it comes to the assertions you use in your tests is that the kind of assertions you use makes a difference in how understandable the test failures will be.

Consider these two assertions verifying the same condition:

```
XCTAssertTrue(sections.count == 1)
XCTAssertEqual(sections.count, 1)
```

If the `sections` array has more than one element, the first will fail with

`XCTAssertTrue failed`

while the second will fail with

`XCTAssertEqual failed: ("1") is not equal to ("2")`

Which one do you think better represents that the array count was not the expected one?

The way a test fails is the starting point to fix the issue that caused the failure. The clearer you can make the test failure, the easier it will be to find its cause.

Don't Let the Tests Crash

We only have one test left to write: the one for the happy path behavior.

The previous tests helped us define the scaffold for the final behavior – the types and method signature makeup. We can now focus on the core logic itself.

The task is to verify that, given an array with items from different categories, the function returns one section per category. To do so, we can use the same approach as the previous tests:

```
func testMenuWithManyCategoriesReturnsOneSectionPerCategory() {
    let menu = [
        MenuItem(category: "pastas", name: "a pasta"),
        MenuItem(category: "drinks", name: "a drink"),
        MenuItem(category: "pastas", name: "another pasta"),
        MenuItem(category: "desserts", name: "a dessert"),
    ]

    let sections = groupMenuByCategory(menu)
```

```
XCTAssertEqual(sections.count, 3)
// How can we verify that there is one section per category?
}
```

Similarly to the previous test, asserting that `sections.count` is equal to 3 is not enough to verify the complete behavior. How can we make sure that the three `MenuSection`s hold a different category each?

How does a `MenuSection` differ from another? `MenuSection` will be used to render each category in the view. It should have a property holding the name of the category:

```
XCTAssertEqual(sections[0].category, "pastas")
                    // Compiler says: Value of type 'MenuSection'
                    // has no member 'category'

XCTAssertEqual(sections[1].category, "drinks")
                    // Compiler says: Value of type 'MenuSection'
                    // has no member 'category'

XCTAssertEqual(sections[2].category, "desserts")
                    // Compiler says: Value of type 'MenuSection'
                    // has no member 'category'
```

Should we also add assertions for the content of each of the sections? Doing so would make the test even more thorough, but it also feels like duplicated work considering we're already testing that all the items of a given category are part of the section for that category in the previous test. If we'll break that expectation while working on the final piece of the implementation, that test will tell us.

The compiler is telling us we need to add category to MenuSection:

```
struct MenuSection {
    let category: String
    let items: [MenuItem]
}
```

With this change, the compilation now fails in the groupMenuByCategory function:

```
return [MenuSection(items: menu)]
    // Compiler says:
    // Missing argument for parameter 'category' in call
```

The simplest thing we can do to make the compilation succeed is to put a hardcoded value:

```
return [MenuSection(category: "", items: menu)]
```

The code compiles, but the test crashes:

```
XCTAssertEqual(sections.count, 3)
XCTAssertEqual(sections[0].category, "pastas")
XCTAssertEqual(sections[1].category, "drinks")
    // Xcode says:
    // Thread 1: Fatal error: Index out of range
XCTAssertEqual(sections[2].category, "desserts")
```

When our tests crash, we lose valuable information. The code we have right now returns only one section, so when we try to access the object at index 1, we crash, but Xcode doesn't report a test failure on the assertion for section.count. While the crash itself could be seen as a test failure, the more information about a failure we have, the easier it becomes to address it.

To avoid index out-of-range crashes in my tests, I like to add this extension for safe subscript access:

```
// Collection+Safe.swift
extension Collection {
    /// Returns the element at the given index if it is within
    /// range, otherwise nil.
    subscript(safe index: Index) -> Element? {
        return indices.contains(index) ? self[index] : nil
    }
}
```

Using the safe subscript, if the index is out of range, we'll get `nil`, which will make the test fail but not crash:

```
XCTAssertEqual(sections.count, 3)
    // XCTAssertEqual failed:
    // ("1") is not equal to ("3")
XCTAssertEqual(sections[safe: 0]?.category, "pastas")
    // XCTAssertEqual failed:
    // ("Optional("")") is not equal to ("Optional("pastas")")
XCTAssertEqual(sections[safe: 1]?.category, "drinks")
    // XCTAssertEqual failed:
    // ("nil") is not equal to ("Optional("drinks")")
XCTAssertEqual(sections[safe: 2]?.category, "desserts")
    // XCTAssertEqual failed:
    // ("nil") is not equal to ("Optional("desserts")")
```

The test failures tell us that our code is returning only one `MenuSection` and with the wrong `category` value. To make the test pass, we need to write the production logic to group the items into sections by category.

We can group elements of an `Array` using a given criterion by using this handy `Dictionary` initializer:

Dictionary(grouping: menu, by: { $0.category })

Once we have a dictionary grouping our MenuItems by their category, we can transform each key-value pair into a MenuSection:

MenuSection(category: key, items: value)

Dictionary doesn't guarantee the order of its keys, so we also need to enforce an order for our sections.

Alberto's menu categories are, *conveniently*, in reverse alphabetical order: starters, pastas, drinks, desserts. We can adopt that for now; we'll add logic for a custom sorting strategy if the need for it emerges as we progress with the app development.

Putting it all together

```
func groupMenuByCategory(_ menu: [MenuItem]) -> [MenuSection] {
    guard menu.isEmpty == false else { return [] }

    return Dictionary(grouping: menu, by: { $0.category })
        .map { key, value in
            MenuSection(category: key, items: value)
        }
        .sorted { $0.category > $1.category }
}
```

Test Naming Conventions

A test method's name should always reflect the behavior it verifies. Because we refined the behavior by introducing the reverse alphabetical ordering, it would be appropriate to update the test name:

```
func testMenuWithManyCategoriesReturnsAsManySectionsIn
ReverseAlphabeticalOrder()
```

Admittedly, that's a *long* method name. Naming things is one of the most complex parts of programming, and tests are no exception.

Using specific test names makes the test output in the console informative, which helps inspect it outside of Xcode, such as in a Continuous Integration service.

The lack of support for annotating tests with descriptions that would appear in the test output is an unfortunate XCTest limitation.

One compromise is to do like Apple does in the few examples available in the XCTest documentation and use less specific test names complemented by a documentation comment:

```
/// Given a menu with many categories, returns as many
/// sections, in reverse alphabetical order
func testMenuWithManyCategories()
```

Swift documentation comments differ from standard comments because they start with /// and support markdown formatting. Tools that generate documentation will look for comments starting with /// and skip those beginning with //.

Apple's approach trades clarity in the test output for test method names that are less verbose.

Another option is to use the popular convention Roy Osherove recommends in *The Art of Unit Testing* and name our tests following the formula

```
[UnitOfWorkName]_[ScenarioUnderTest]_[ExpectedBehavior]
```

Keeping in mind that XCTest needs the test prefix to identify a method as a test to run, the name in our example would become

```
func test_groupMenuByCategory_MenuWithManyCategories_ReturnsAs
ManySectionsInReverseAlphabeticalOrder()
```

That's *even longer* than the one we began with! However, the underscores break the name up and make it easier to parse for some readers. If you can get past the awkwardness of mixing camel casing

(FooBar) with snake casing (foo_bar), this naming convention can help readers navigate your tests.

Yet another option is to adopt the open source library Quick, which provides a DSL to describe test methods using strings. Appendix B includes an overview of how to write tests using Quick.

Each of the options we just discussed has its merits and its tradeoffs. Each could be an excellent fit for a project and a poor fit for another.

When working in a team, individuals may have different preferred styles, but it's crucial to choose one and stick with it. Consistency removes the mental overhead of having to parse the code's structure to get to its meaning, making the path to understanding shorter for both your teammates and your future self.

In this book, we'll keep naming our test methods with plain camel casing. That's not a judgment call on this particular style over the others, but an attempt to keep the test and production code homogeneous to add less overhead to what we're trying to learn.

Red, Green, and Don't Forget Refactor

All the tests are passing now, but we are not done yet. It's time to ask whether we can improve the code.

Let's take a look at the production code:

```swift
func groupMenuByCategory(_ menu: [MenuItem]) -> [MenuSection] {
    guard menu.isEmpty == false else { return [] }

    return Dictionary(grouping: menu, by: { $0.category })
        .map { key, value in
            MenuSection(category: key, items: value)
        }
        .sorted { $0.category > $1.category }
}
```

Since we are manipulating sequences, there is no need to check whether the input is empty before processing it. With an empty array as input, the sequence manipulation will still run on it but won't manipulate anything, producing an empty array as the output.

Here's the final version of our function:

```
func groupMenuByCategory(_ menu: [MenuItem]) -> [MenuSection] {
    return Dictionary(grouping: menu, by: { $0.category })
        .map { key, value in
            MenuSection(category: key, items: value)
        }
        .sorted { $0.category > $1.category }
}
```

If we rerun the tests, they are still green.

Once you have your unit tests lattice, experimenting with the production code implementation details becomes easy: make the change you want to try, and then if the tests still pass, you can be confident nothing broke.

We now have a little kernel of pure business logic, which we know works because we've seen its tests go from red to green as we built it. Let's hook it up with the UI.

Wiring Up the UI

When building applications in the Apple ecosystem, there are two options to write UI code: the recent SwiftUI or the older UIKit, WatchKit, and AppKit. You can mix and match between the two, but we'll be working with SwiftUI only in this book.

SwiftUI is still young – as I'm writing this chapter, not even two years have passed since its introduction at WWDC 2019 – but there is not doubt it is how we'll be building user interfaces in the years to come.

The testing strategies that we'll learn apply to the older frameworks too. If you want to know more about TDD and UIKit, head over to Appendix C.

There isn't a straightforward way to write unit tests for SwiftUI views. We'll learn more about why that's the case and why it shouldn't concern for us in Chapters 6 and 7.

For the moment, we just need to observe that all the logic to generate the content of our view is already defined in groupMenuByCategory(_:). We don't need a test to guide us in implementing the menu view because the only thing we have to do is describe the layout in SwiftUI and feed it the groupMenuByCategory(_:) return value. Having views free from presentation or behavior logic makes them straightforward to write and allows you to build that logic elsewhere using TDD.

Here's the view implementation:

```swift
// MenuList.swift
import SwiftUI

struct MenuList: View {
    let sections: [MenuSection]

    var body: some View {
        List {
            ForEach(sections) { section in
                Section(header: Text(section.category)) {
                    ForEach(section.items) { item in
                        Text(item.name)
                    }
                }
            }
        }
    }
}
```

To make `MenuItem` and `MenuSection` work in the `ForEach`, we need to conform them to `Identifiable`:

```swift
// MenuItem.swift
extension MenuItem: Identifiable {
    var id: String { name }
}

// MenuSection.swift
extension MenuSection: Identifiable {
    var id: String { category }
}
```

Finally, we can bring it all together in the root SwiftUI App:

```swift
// AlbertosApp.swift
import SwiftUI

@main
struct AlbertosApp: App {

    var body: some Scene {
        WindowGroup {
            NavigationView {
                MenuList(sections: groupMenuByCategory(menu))
                    .navigationTitle("Alberto's ▮")
            }
        }
    }
}

// In this first iteration the menu is an hard-coded array
let menu = [
    MenuItem(category: "starters", name: "Caprese Salad"),
    MenuItem(category: "starters", name: "Arancini Balls"),
    MenuItem(category: "pastas", name: "Penne all'Arrabbiata"),
```

```
    MenuItem(category: "pastas", name: "Spaghetti Carbonara"),
    MenuItem(category: "drinks", name: "Water"),
    MenuItem(category: "drinks", name: "Red Wine"),
    MenuItem(category: "desserts", name: "Tiramisù"),
    MenuItem(category: "desserts", name: "Crema Catalana"),
]
```

In Figure 4-1, you can see how the SwiftUI code renders in the Simulator.

Figure 4-1. *The SwiftUI view rendered in the iPhone Simulator with the fake data*

Pure Functions

The functions we worked on in this and the previous chapter have two things in common:

1. If called with the same inputs, they return the same result every time. That's because they don't track internal state between calls, nor do they take into account any external state (e.g., the date at the time of calling).

2. They have no side effects. There is no change in the app state whether you call the function once, twice, or never.

Functions with these properties equate to functions in the mathematical sense. As such, we call them *pure* functions.

Pure functions are your best friends. Because their output depends only on their input (property 1), a test for them requires only an input that will produce your desired output. And because they don't alter the state of the program that calls them (property 2), you can exercise them without having to do any state management in the test case (see "XCTestCase Life Cycle" in Chapter 2).

Unfortunately, we cannot build a whole app only with pure functions. At some point, we'll have to interface with some stateful component like a database or the network.

Still, we can try to implement as much logic as possible into pure functions and only have a thin *impure* layer gluing them together. The pressure of writing tests first pushes you to do exactly that.

We built a working app without ever launching it in the Simulator, using tests to get faster feedback instead.

Because we decomposed the problem in small pieces, we now have something that stands on its own, even though far from finished. We can share it with our client as a sign of early progress. This allows us to make the feedback loop with them faster, the same way as we did with our code.

In the next chapter, we'll look at a technique to keep our test clean and focused and allow us to iterate on the types that make up the app with ease.

Key Takeaways

- **Partition Problems and Solve Sequentially**: Apps are made of features; features are made of objects collaborating together; objects are made of methods and types that can be looked at in isolation.

- **Build the behavior starting from the edge cases**. This allows you to build up the foundation on which the complete implementation will stand.

- **Use the strictest and clearest assertions possible in your tests**. They will give you clearer feedback on what to build next and make triaging test failure in the future easier.

- **Don't let your tests crash**. When the tests crash, you lose valuable information. Use techniques like XCTUnwrap and safe Collection subscript access to avoid crashes.

- **Pure functions are easy to test because they have no external dependencies and no side effects**. Writing tests first helps you think in terms of pure functions.

- **Keep the SwiftUI layer behavior-free**. Keep logic away from the SwiftUI View, so that you can work and iterate on it with the faster test-driven feedback loop.

CHAPTER 5

Changing Tests with Fixtures

How can you modify the type signatures of your production code without having to update the tests that consume them too?

By decoupling the tests from the production object initialization code.

Test-Driven Development promises to help developers work at a steady pace. For this to happen, writing tests first is not enough; we need to maintain the test code like the production one, keep it nimble and simple to work with. As Robert C. Martin puts it in *Clean Code: A Handbook of Agile Software Craftsmanship*

> Test code is just as important as production code.
> It is not a second-class citizen. It requires thought,
> design, and care. It must be kept as clean as
> production code.

This chapter introduces a technique that allows you to update the shape of your production types without having to constantly go back and update your tests: the *fixture*.

We'll see what fixtures are, how to define them for our types, and how this approach can help us write tests that are not only simpler to maintain but also clearer to read.

© Gio Lodi 2021
G. Lodi, *Test-Driven Development in Swift*, https://doi.org/10.1007/978-1-4842-7002-8_5

The Hidden Cost of Source Changes

Alberto was excited to receive the early version of the app we built in the previous chapter and sent some feedback. Something important for his menu is to show which items are spicy. He doesn't want his customers to order a dish they won't end up enjoying because they don't like hot food.[1]

Alberto wants a visual hint next to each spicy item, like in his paper menu. You agree to start with a chili emoji, 🌶. (Emojis are a great way to add color and simulate icons when you don't have access to a designer or time to draw them.)

To make this change, you'll need to update the data model to track whether a MenuItem is spicy and also update the UI layer to add the visual hint for those items that are spicy. Let's look at the data model first. We'll think about the view in the next chapter.

We can update MenuItem to add spiciness information like this:

```swift
// MenuItem.swift
struct MenuItem {
    let name: String
    let category: String
    let spicy: Bool
}
```

If we make that change, we'll get a bunch of compilation failures with this error:

```
MenuItem(category: "pastas", name: "name")
  // Compiler says: Missing argument for parameter 'spicy' in call
```

The new property in MenuItem means the compiler will generate a new initializer, making the one we used before invalid.

To go back to the green state, we'd need to update all the call sites where we instantiate MenuItem. Doing so scales linearly with the number of instantiations: the more we have, the more work it will be to update them. You might not have a lot of updates to do in the production code, where usually a type is instantiated only a handful of times, but in the tests we may have dozens of calls to the init method.

Unit tests are meant to save developers' time; if maintaining the test code becomes a time-consuming task, Test-Driven Development goes from being your productivity's best ally to its worst enemy.

We need a way to decouple how we create values in the tests from their actual init, so we can update the init without having to always touch all of the initializations in the tests.

Fixtures

To keep the cost of updating the MenuItem init low, we can make the tests initialize it in a centralized location, so that every time its shape changes, we only have to update one piece of code.

We can extend MenuItem in the test target to provide a static method the tests can use to get an instance of the type. This approach is known as fixture, and because we define the fixture in an extension, this technique is called *Fixture Extension*:

```
// MenuItem+Fixture.swift
@testable import Albertos

extension MenuItem {
```

```swift
    static func fixture(
        category: String = "category",
        name: String = "name"
    ) -> MenuItem {
        MenuItem(category: category, name: name)
    }
}
```

What keeps the effort of updating the test suite low are the default values of all the input parameters.

When you add a new property, you only need to update the fixture and provide a default value. You won't need to update any of the existing tests, and you'll be able to use the fixture with the new property when writing new tests that need it. When you remove a property, the only tests that will need an update are those passing a custom value to it in the fixture invocation.

We can update our tests to use fixtures like this:

```swift
// MenuGroupingTests.swift
func testMenuWithOneCategoryReturnsOneSection() throws {
    let menu = [
        MenuItem.fixture(category: "pastas", name: "name"),
        MenuItem.fixture(category: "pastas", name: "other name"),
    ]

    let sections = groupMenuByCategories(menu)

    XCTAssertEqual(sections.count, 1)
    let section = try XCTUnwrap(sections.first)
    XCTAssertEqual(section.items.count, 2)
    XCTAssertEqual(section.items.first,  "name")
    XCTAssertEqual(section.items.last, "other name")
}
```

Now, to add the spicy property, the only code that we need to change is in the fixture definition:

```swift
// MenuItem.swift
struct MenuItem {
    let name: String
    let category: String
    let spicy: Bool
}
```

```swift
// MenuItem+Fixture.swift
extension MenuItem {

    static func fixture(
        category: String = "category",
        name: String = "name",
        spicy: Bool = false,
    ) -> MenuItem {
        MenuItem(
            category: category,
            name: name,
            spicy: spicy
        )
    }
}
```

Fixtures vs. Convenience Initializers

Why defining a fixture instead of a convenience initializer with default values? Because of clarity.

When reading `let item = MenuItem.fixture(name: "a name")`, the fact that the instance comes with default values chosen for the purpose of testing is much clearer than if we were reading `let item = MenuItem(name: "a name")`. Calling `MenuItem(...)` looks like production code; `MenuItem.fixture(...)` is something that belongs to the test suite.

Making your code clear to read has a huge return on investment: you write your code once, but you and your teammates will read it many times over. This is true for test and production code alike.

Fixtures Make the Test Actors Explicit

Once you have your fixtures in place, you can write clearer tests by focusing only on the input elements that actually affect the behavior under test.

Let's take a look at this test from the previous chapter, written without using fixtures:

```
func testMenuWithManyCategoriesReturnsOneSectionPerCategory
InReverseAlphabeticalOrder() {
    let menu = [
        MenuItem(
            category: "pastas", name: "a pasta", spicy: false
        ),
        MenuItem(
            category: "drinks", name: "a drink", spicy: false
        ),
        MenuItem(
            category: "pastas", name: "another pasta", spicy: false
        ),
        MenuItem(
            category: "desserts", name: "a dessert", spicy: false
        ),
    ]
```

```
let sections = groupMenuByCategories(menu)

XCTAssertEqual(sections.count, 3)
XCTAssertEqual(sections[0].category,  "pastas")
XCTAssertEqual(sections[1].category,  "drinks")
XCTAssertEqual(sections[2].category, "desserts")
}
```

We're testing whether the generated sections match the input categories and are in reverse alphabetical order. Of all the properties of the input, the only one that affects the output is category. The code we have to prepare the input, though, has to add values for all of the other irrelevant properties.

Using fixtures, we can remove the noise, keeping the input focused only on what really matters:

```
let menu = [
  MenuItem.fixture(category: "pastas"),
  MenuItem.fixture(category: "drinks"),
  MenuItem.fixture(category: "pastas"),
  MenuItem.fixture(category: "dessert")
]
```

Bonus tip   You can make the code more compact by defining the type of the array and then omitting the MenuItem when calling the function; the Swift compiler infers it.

```
let menu: [MenuItem] = [
  .fixture(category: "pastas"),
  .fixture(category: "drinks"),
  .fixture(category: "pastas"),
  .fixture(category: "dessert")
]
```

Alongside making your tests clearer to the reader and removing the friction in changing the source code, fixtures also save you time when writing the tests themselves. You don't have to think about the values for properties that are irrelevant to the behavior under test nor type them.

Fixtures Are Composable

You can use fixtures to define new fixtures. For example, here's how to define a fixture for MenuSection:

```
// MenuSection+Fixture.swift
@testable import Albertos

extension MenuSection {

    static func fixture(
        category: String = "a category",
        items: [MenuItem] = [.fixture()]
    ) -> MenuSection {
        return MenuSection(category: category, items: items)
    }
}
```

Introduce Fixtures As Early As Possible

Introducing fixtures is like saving for retirement; the sooner you start, the more value you'll get out of them because of the compounding effect.

Defining a fixture for a type and adopting it in your existing tests slows you down in the short term, but you'll quickly make up for it when you need to change the shape of that type.

The *rule of three* is a good heuristic to decide when to introduce fixtures. If you already called the `init` of a type in two tests, define a fixture for it before calling in a third.

Practice Time

To experience the value of fixtures firsthand, add new properties to `MenuItem`. For example, we'll need a property for the price of the dishes later in the development. Try adding it and see what you need to change in the production and test code:

```
// MenuItem.swift
struct MenuItem {
    let name: String
    let category: String
    let spicy: Bool
    let price: Double
}
```

Key Takeaways

- **Use a Fixture Extension to remove friction when updating the shape of a production code type**. By adding a layer of indirection between how you create values in the tests and their `init`, you won't need to update every test call site when you edit, add, or remove properties from a type.

- **Fixtures help you keep your tests focused on the key actors**. Thanks to their default values, fixtures allow you to omit `init` parameters that do not affect the behavior you are testing.

- **Fixtures are composable**. You can use a fixture as the default value for a property of another fixture.

- **Introduce fixtures early**. The time-saving value of fixtures compounds over time; you can adopt the rule of three heuristic to know when to add them.

Endnote

1. One could argue that adding a UI hint for spicy food is not top priority at this point of the development and that we should focus on building out the skeleton of functionality around which the app will revolve, such as networking APIs and ordering items. Absolutely true! From the point of view of learning how to test-drive the implementation of an iOS app, though, it's useful to learn how to write unit tests for the logic that generates the data for the UI before moving forward with more advanced topics.

CHAPTER 6

Testing Static SwiftUI Views

How do you use Test-Driven Development for the view layer when there is no straightforward way to test SwiftUI views?

By extracting all the view configuration logic in a dedicated object and test that instead.

Xcode Previews and manual testing are not the only ways to make sure your views behave correctly. In this chapter, we'll learn how to use tests to guide us in implementing the view behavior. The key is to make the view *humble* and free from any logic and have it ask what to show to an object that is not tied to SwiftUI, one we can easily implement test-first. We'll call this object *ViewModel* and look at how to build it for two of our views.

The Problem with Presentation Logic in the View

In the previous chapter, we added a spicy property to MenuItem to start implementing Alberto's request of having a visual hint to indicate which items are spicy. The first iteration of the UI for this feature can be a simple chili emoji: 🌶.

It might be tempting to add the required presentation logic in the existing MenuList code, from this

```
Text(item.name)
```

to this

```
Text(item.spicy ? "\(item.name) 🌶": item.name)
```

The first concern with this approach is a practical one: embedding presentation logic in the view layer can quickly bloat it, making it harder to read. The code to add a spiciness indicator is a one-liner, but that's not always the case; there might be an enum to switch on or multiple values to read.

Even if you weren't bothered by bloated view files, there is the question of how to test this code. As of this writing, Apple does not provide a straightforward way of writing unit tests for SwiftUI views, encouraging developers to iterate on them using Xcode Previews instead.

Previews are an excellent feedback mechanism for how the layout you're writing looks like, but they cannot tell you if the logic is correct with the same level of detail as a test.

Writing tests for SwiftUI views is inconvenient because the only outlet we have to inspect them is their *opaque* body property. We may define a view like this:

```
import SwiftUI

struct ExampleView: View {

    var body: some View {
        VStack {
            Text("Title").bold()
            Text("Subtitle")
        }
    }
}
```

But when we access the body property at runtime, it's a much more complex object:[1]

```
VStack<TupleView<(Text, Text)>>(_tree: SwiftUI._VariadicView.
Tree<SwiftUI._VStackLayout, ...
```

This might seem a limitation, but the framework's declarative philosophy makes it unnecessary for a consumer to ever worry about the content of the body.

"Views are a function of state, not a sequence of events," explains Luca Bernardi, one of the SwiftUI engineers at Apple, in the *Data Flow Through SwiftUI* WWDC 2019 session. SwiftUI unidirectional data flow architecture is such that the only knob developers can turn to affect the view is the state they feed it as input.

There is little value in writing tests that inspect the view itself because the body's runtime value is an implementation detail of how SwiftUI works. As long as we play by the rules of the framework, we can trust that if we supply a view with a correct state, it will render on screen as intended.

SwiftUI doesn't limit testability. It enhances it! It makes it simpler and secure to apply *Partition Problem and Solve Sequentially*.

Decouple Presentation Logic from the View Implementation

In the preceding inline approach, MenuList is in charge of two things: defining the menu row layout and deciding whether to add each item's spiciness indicator. It has two responsibilities. It's solving two problems.

The layout definition is a problem that lives in the SwiftUI domain; MenuList is the best place to solve it. However, the presentation logic evaluating whether to add the 🌶 symbol has no reason to be tied to the SwiftUI framework: we can build it in isolation.

Giving `MenuList` responsibility for both defining the layout and deciding its content blows up its self-esteem. We'd better make it humble[2] and only take care of what it's best suited for: defining the layout.

To put `MenuList`'s ambition in check, we can extract the logic to decide what content it should display in a dedicated object that we can build using TDD. Once completed, we'll make `MenuList` ask this new component what to show.

Preparatory Refactor: Reduce the Working Surface Area

Adding the spiciness hint is a change at the individual menu row level, but our only access to the rows is through `MenuList`. To make our job easier, let's refactor the view to isolate the part we need to work on:

```swift
// MenuList.swift
import SwiftUI

struct MenuList: View {

    let sections: [MenuSection]

    var body: some View {
        List {
            ForEach(sections) { section in
                Section(header: Text(section.category)) {
                    ForEach(section.items) { item in
                        MenuRow(item: item)
                    }
                }
            }
        }
    }
}
```

```
// MenuRow.swift
import SwiftUI

struct MenuRow: View {

    let item: MenuItem

    var body: some View {
        Text(item.name)
    }
}
```

Reducing the code's surface area makes it easier to reason about and manipulate.

Since we don't have any test for the view – yet – the only way we have to check that this refactor succeeded is to look at the Xcode Preview or launch the app.

ViewModel

The next step is to write a test for the object in which we'll move the presentation logic for the MenuRow. How should we call this?

ViewModel is a popular name for this kind of object. The term comes from the MVVM pattern for building UI applications introduced by Microsoft in 2005 and represents the "Model of a View, [...] a specialization of the Model that the View can use for data-binding."

An alternative name could be Presentation Model, as defined by Martin Fowler. I tend to prefer ViewModel, especially because of the data-binding capabilities that SwiftUI offers – more on those in the next chapter.

As usual, let's start with the test list:

```
// MenuRowViewModelTests.swift
@testable import Albertos
```

```
import XCTest

class MenuRowViewModelTests: XCTestCase {

    func testWhenItemIsNotSpicyTextIsItemNameOnly() {}

    func testWhenItemIsSpicyTextIsItemNameWithChiliEmoji() {}
}
```

What's the simplest scenario to tackle first? The one where we don't have to do any extra work:

```
func testWhenItemIsNotSpicyTextIsItemNameOnly() {
    let item = MenuItem.fixture(name: "name", spicy: false)
    let viewModel = MenuRow.ViewModel(item: item)
        // Compiler says:
        // Type 'MenuRow' has no member 'ViewModel'
    XCTAssertEqual(viewModel.text, "name")
}
```

The compiler points out that there is no ViewModel type yet. Because a ViewModel is tied to a single view, using a nested type makes the one-to-one relationship clear. Of course, a standalone MenuRowViewModel would do as well.

When using the nested type approach, we should still place the ViewModel in a dedicated file, to make it easier to find it when using Xcode's Open Quickly functionality:

```
// MenuRow.ViewModel.swift
extension MenuRow {

    struct ViewModel {

        let text: String

        init(item: MenuItem) {
            text = ""
```

```
      }
    }
}
```

The first test now compiles but fails because of the empty string we set as the text value.

Let's make the test pass by updating the MenuRow.ViewModel init to

```
init(item: MenuItem) {
    text = item.name
}
```

Now, let's write a test for the chili addition:

```
func testWhenItemIsSpicyTextIsItemNameWithChiliEmoji() {
    let item = MenuItem.fixture(name: "name", spicy: true)
    let viewModel = MenuRow.ViewModel(item: item)
    XCTAssertEqual(viewModel.text, "name 🌶")
}
```

The test fails. We can recycle the ternary operator from the start of this chapter to make it pass and complete the implementation:

```
init(item: MenuItem) {
    text = item.spicy ? "\(item.name) 🌶": item.name
}
```

We're in the green state. Is there any refactor we could apply to improve the implementation? Nothing comes to mind, so let's proceed to wire the ViewModel to its view.

Using the ViewModel in the View

It's time to update the body result builder to read from the ViewModel. This will keep the view humble, entrusting all the presentation logic to its ViewModel instance:

```
// MenuRow.swift
struct MenuRow: View {

    let viewModel: ViewModel

    var body: some View {
        Text(viewModel.text)
    }
}

// MenuList.swift
struct MenuList: View {

    let sections: [MenuSection]

    var body: some View {
        List {
            ForEach(sections) { section in
                Section(header: Text(section.category)) {
                    ForEach(section.items) { item in
                        MenuRow(viewModel: .init(item: item))
                    }
                }
            }
        }
    }
}
```

Figure 6-1 shows the menu list with the spiciness indicator.

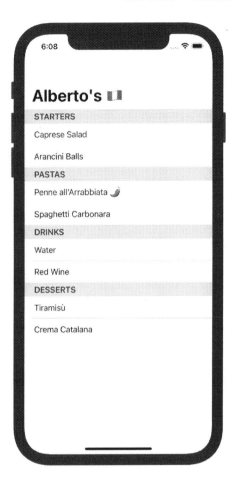

Figure 6-1. *The menu list rendered in the iPhone Simulator with the spiciness indicator*

Beyond Testability

Thanks to MenuRow.ViewModel, we implemented the conditional logic to show the spiciness visual hint to the user in isolation and with the tests' feedback to guide us. Once again, we only had to run the app at the end of the implementation process as a final check to ensure everything was wired up together.

The view itself still doesn't have a dedicated test, but there's not much that can go wrong in there. Because it's behavior-free, the only mistake that can happen is reading from the wrong `ViewModel` property, something that's relatively easy to spot.

With the ViewModel already in place, we'll be able to use TDD for any new presentation detail in `MenuRow` with no extra setup cost.

The decoupling also means that we can tinker with the UI layout easily because it's streamlined and free from bulky behavioral code.

Separating presentation logic from layout implementation enables parallelization when working in a team. Given a specification for a view, two developers can pair to define its `ViewModel` properties and then work side by side. One can implement the presentation logic that sets those properties with TDD, the other can define the `View` layout using the feedback-driven Xcode Preview process.

The extra code we had to write to wedge the `ViewModel` between the SwiftUI view and the data model will pay off over time. Types are cheap. Working in a codebase made up of many little highly cohesive, loosely coupled objects is far more pleasurable than dealing with a few huge components containing all of the code.

ViewModels Everywhere!

View models allow us to decouple the presentation logic from the layout definition. Having the logic live in a standalone object makes the code easier to test and modify because there are no ties to the SwiftUI implementation requirements or the UIKit views' life cycle.

If your view does anything more than a 1-to-1 displaying of data from a model object, you should have a ViewModel for it.

We know the menu list view will need more complicated behavior than loading a static list of sections. While decomposing the minimum viable feature set in Chapter 4, we established the menu will likely come from a source such as a file or a remote API.

Now it's the best time to refactor `MenuList` to use a ViewModel.

Since `MenuList` displays sections, its ViewModel should take care of generating those sections. That is, `MenuList.ViewModel` should expose a `sections` property for `MenuList` to read the same way `MenuRow.ViewModel` exposes a `text` property for `MenuRow`.

One option could be to move the responsibility of calling `groupMenuByCategory` from the SwiftUI app implementation to `MenuList.ViewModel`. We could update the existing tests for the function to instantiate a view model and read its `section` property, renaming them from `MenuGroupingTests` to `MenuListViewModelTests`.

A different approach could be moving the menu grouping logic into a dedicated object instead and pass that to `MenuList.ViewModel`. This would simplify the job of testing the ViewModel: we'd simply need to verify it uses the given object to generate the sections.

Yet another approach, the one I want to show you, is using *Function Injection*. Because functions are first-class citizens in Swift, we can use them as arguments for other functions. This way, we can build a ViewModel agnostic of the grouping implementation details by making it ask for a closure to call to generate the sections.

DEPENDENCY INJECTION

When learning about software design and testing, the term Dependency Injection, or DI, eventually comes up. It may sound daunting, but, as James Shore puts it, Dependency Injection "is a 25-dollar term for a 5-cent concept."

Injecting dependencies simply means passing them as values to the objects or methods that need them, as opposed to getting a hold of the dependencies in the objects or methods themselves. When a component explicitly asks for all of its dependencies, it's interface becomes honest, and a reader of the code won't be surprised by a hidden side effect.

While there are frameworks that allow runtime dependency injection, they come with such configuration overhead that is worth the investment only in a few cases.

Function Injection is a case of DI where the dependency is encapsulated in a single function.

Here's how to write a test that leverages Function Injection:

```
// MenuList.ViewModelTests.swift
@testable import Albertos
import XCTest

class MenuListViewModelTests: XCTestCase {

    func testCallsGivenGroupingFunction() {
        var called = false
        let inputSections = [MenuSection.fixture()]
        let spyClosure: ([MenuItem]) -> [MenuSection] = { items in
            called = true
            return inputSections
        }

        let viewModel = MenuList.ViewModel(menu: [.fixture()],
            menuGrouping: spyClosure)
        let sections = viewModel.sections

        // Check that the given closure was called
        XCTAssertTrue(called)
        // Check that the returned value was built with the
        // closure
        XCTAssertEqual(sections, inputSections)
    }
}
```

This test checks MenuList.ViewModel's behavior by using a "spy" closure. The closure sets a flag when called and returns a constant value. We can then assert the ViewModel uses the closure to generate the sections by checking that the flag became true and the returned value is the one from the closure. We'll talk more about spying on our code in Chapter 12.

For the XCTAssertEqual on [MenuSection] to work, we need to make both MenuSection and MenuItem conform to Equatable:

```
// MenuItem.swift
extension MenuItem: Equatable {}
```

```
// MenuSection.swift
extension MenuSection: Equatable {}
```

Here's an implementation of MenuList.ViewModel that makes the test pass:

```
// MenuList.ViewModel.swift

extension MenuList {

    struct ViewModel {

        let sections: [MenuSection]

        init(
            menu: [MenuItem],
            menuGrouping: @escaping ([MenuItem]) ->
            [MenuSection] = groupMenuByCategory
        ) {
            self.sections = menuGrouping(menu)
        }
    }
}
```

The combination of Function Injection and Swift's default parameter values means callers in the production code don't need to concern themselves with what value to pass to menuGrouping.

The final step is updating MenuList to use its ViewModel and AlbertosApp to provide MenuList with one:

```
// MenuList.swift
import SwiftUI

struct MenuList: View {

    let viewModel: ViewModel

    var body: some View {
        List {
            ForEach(viewModel.sections) { section in
                Section(header: Text(section.category)) {
                    ForEach(section.items) { item in
                        MenuRow(viewModel: .init(item: item))
                    }
                }
            }
        }
    }
}

// AlbertosApp.swift
@main
struct AlbertosApp: App {
```

```
var body: some Scene {
    WindowGroup {
        NavigationView {
            MenuList(viewModel: .init(menu: menu))
                .navigationTitle("Alberto's ▨")
        }
    }
}
}
```

Function Injection is useful to decouple an object that needs to coordinate different behaviors from the implementation details of such behaviors. ViewModels often take up that coordination role; they are the *glue* between the view and the different business logic components that provide the data to show.

This approach might seem overkill right now but will come in handy once MenuList.ViewModel becomes responsible for coordinating between the view and the data loading logic.

We've seen how using the ViewModel pattern allows us to keep SwiftUI views focused only on the layout and have pure Swift objects responsible for the presentation logic. Because SwiftUI views are a function of state, the framework marries perfectly with TDD. You write the logic to provide the input test-first to guarantee its correctness, and SwiftUI ensures the output on screen will be consistent.

The ViewModels we built in this chapter are both static, but that's seldom the case. Most applications load data from one or more sources and update their views with it. The data and the view change over time.

Apple's Combine framework provides the tools to manage the flow of data over time elegantly and with tight integration with SwiftUI. In the next chapter, we'll see how to evolve our ViewModels to handle dynamic changes in the app's state.

Key Takeaways

- **The view doesn't have to be responsible for deciding both *how* to show data and *what* data to show**. It can be humble and only declare the layout while delegating the presentation logic.

- **Use a `ViewModel` to hold all the presentation logic**. By detaching it from the SwiftUI implementation, you can use TDD like on any other business logic object.

- **Make the `View` ask the `ViewModel` what to show**. This keeps the view focused on layout only, a perfect fit for quickly iterating with Xcode Previews.

- **Use Function Injection to isolate nontrivial behavior from components depending on it**. This lets you use the ViewModel as a coordination layer only, making it easier to add more functionality to it and its view.

- **Many isolated objects doing only one thing each are easier to work with than a few interdependent ones doing many things each**.

Endnotes

1. For reference, here's the full printout of the body via po in the Xcode console with lldb:

```
▽ VStack<TupleView<(Text, Text)>>
  ▽ _tree : Tree<_VStackLayout, TupleView<(Text,
    Text)>>
    ▽ root : _VStackLayout
```

```
▽ alignment : HorizontalAlignment
  ▽ key : AlignmentKey
    - bits : 140735441946104
  - spacing : nil
▽ content : TupleView<(Text, Text)>
  ▽ value : 2 elements
    ▽ .0 : Text
      ▽ storage : Storage
        ▽ anyTextStorage : <LocalizedTextStorage:
          0x600001ab1810>
      ▽ modifiers : 1 element
        ▽ 0 : Modifier
          - anyTextModifier : <BoldText
            Modifier : 0x600003bbe420>
    ▽.1 : Text
      ▽ storage : Storage
        ▽ anyTextStorage : <Localized
          TextStorage : 0x600001ab18b0>
      - modifiers : 0 elements
```

2. The idea of making a hard-to-test object free from
    behavior was introduced by Michael Feathers
    in his paper "The Humble Dialog Box" and then
    formalized into the Humble Object pattern by
    Gerard Meszaros in *xUnit Test Patterns* (p. 695).

CHAPTER 7

Testing Dynamic SwiftUI Views

How do you test the way a view updates when it receives new data?

By wrapping the updates in a @Published property of the ViewModel and test that using asynchronous expectations.

In the previous chapter, we saw that SwiftUI views are hard to test and that the trick is to bypass them, moving all of the presentation logic in a dedicated object, the ViewModel. When all your presentation logic is in the ViewModel, you can test dynamic views as well as static ones.

SwiftUI and Combine let you seamlessly update the view as new data becomes available. You can make the ViewModel *publish* properties using Combine, and, if you subscribe the view to them, SwiftUI will trigger a re-render every time a new value is published.

Because SwiftUI manages the view update, you only need to test that the ViewModel publishes correct values.

In this chapter, we'll look at how to use Test-Driven Development to make a ViewModel expose data with Combine and how to decouple it from the concrete data source using the *Dependency Inversion Principle (DIP)*.

We'll be working with asynchronous code; if you need a reminder on how this mode of execution differs from the synchronous logic we've worked with so far, head over to the "Expectations for Asynchronous Code" section in Chapter 2.

© Gio Lodi 2021
G. Lodi, *Test-Driven Development in Swift*, https://doi.org/10.1007/978-1-4842-7002-8_7

Alberto likes to change his menu frequently, depending on what's in season and what bargains he can get at the produce market. You decide to read the menu from a remote API to update it without requiring a new app version.

Loading the menu from a remote API involves

- Fetching the data from the API via HTTP

- Converting the data from the API response into something the app understands

- Showing the fetched data in the UI

Let's start with the UI work. We'll address the other tasks in the following chapters.

Starting from the user-facing layer is a way to get to an Earliest Testable version of our feature faster, similarly to what we did in Chapter 4. We can share a version of the app dynamically loading dummy data with Alberto to see what he thinks of it. If we built the network component first, we couldn't share it with him because it needs a UI to be exercised by a user.

The code we'll write relies heavily on SwiftUI and Combine. Before getting started, here's a quick overview of how data flows in SwiftUI.

How SwiftUI and Combine Make Seamless View Updates Possible

A major difference between SwiftUI and its predecessors UIKit and AppKit is that its views are immutable. As we've seen in the previous chapter, views are a function of state, not a sequence of events. The state is the single source of truth from which the framework derives the view. Our code cannot directly mutate the view; we can only change the application's state. This SwiftUI trait alone removes the possibility of a whole set of bugs caused by the state held in the view becoming inconsistent.

SwiftUI's immutability marries with Combine's streaming capabilities to provide elegant ways to keep views in sync as data *flows* through.

One tool for asynchronous operations is Combine's `Publisher` type, which can stream new values over time and to which objects can subscribe. A convenient way to create `Publisher`s is to take an object, make it conform to the `ObservableObject` protocol, and use the `@Published` wrapper on one or more of its properties. The wrapper generates a `Publisher` that sends a new value every time the property changes.

And here's where the integration between the two frameworks really shines: SwiftUI provides an `@ObservedObject` property wrapper for types conforming to `ObservableObject`. Every time a `@Published` property of an `@ObservedObject` emits a new value, SwiftUI will automatically trigger a new render of the view.

But enough theory. Let's get coding.

Make the ViewModel Stream Updates with `ObservableObject`

For SwiftUI to do all the heavy lifting of keeping the view in sync with the data we load from the API, we need to provide it an `ObservableObject` that exposes the data through one or more `@Published` properties.

In Chapter 6, we saw how to keep the view free of presentation logic using a ViewModel. The ViewModel is the best candidate to become the view's `@ObservedObject`. It's a natural extension of its duty: from the holder of static data for the view to read to the holder of static and dynamic data for the view to read and sync with.

How should `MenuList.ViewModel` behave when fetching the menu from the remote API? Here's an initial approach:

- When the fetching starts, it should publish an empty [MenuSection].

- If the fetching succeeds, it should publish the received menu converted to [MenuSection] and appropriately grouped.

- If the fetching fails, it should publish an error.

We can translate these requirements into a test list:

```
// MenuList.ViewModelTests.swift
// ...
class MenuList.ViewModelTests: XCTestCase {

    // ...

    func testWhenFetchingStartsPublishesEmptyMenu() {}

    func testWhenFecthingSucceedsPublishesSectionsBuiltFrom
    ReceivedMenuAndGivenGroupingClosure() {}

    func testWhenFetchingFailsPublishesAnError() {}
}
```

Let's start working on the simplest scenario to build up the implementation's foundation:

```
func testWhenFetchingStartsPublishesEmptyMenu() {
    let viewModel = MenuList.ViewModel(menu: [.fixture()])

    XCTAssertTrue(viewModel.sections.isEmpty)
}
```

This test fails, and if we look at the ViewModel's current implementation, it's clear why: MenuList.ViewModel doesn't fetch or publish data yet. The MenuList.ViewModel version we wrote for the static screen uses its init [MenuItem] parameter to generate the sections:

```
// MenuList.ViewModel.swift
extension MenuList {

    struct ViewModel {

        let sections: [MenuSection]

        init(
            menu: [MenuItem],
            menuGrouping: @escaping ([MenuItem]) -> [MenuSection]
            = groupMenuByCategory
        ) {
            self.sections = menuGrouping(menu)
        }
    }
}
```

The simplest thing we can do to make the test pass is to assign the result of calling menuGrouping on an empty array to sections:

```
// MenuList.ViewModel.swift
extension MenuList {

    struct ViewModel {

        let sections: [MenuSection]

        init(
            menu: [MenuItem],
            menuGrouping: @escaping ([MenuItem]) ->
            [MenuSection] = groupMenuByCategory
        ) {
            self.sections = menuGrouping([])
        }
    }
}
```

The change we just made is the *simplest* thing to do, not the *best*. It's a small change that gets our new test to pass, establishing the green baseline against which we can make the more substantial change of removing the [MenuItem] init parameter.

The new test might be green, but the one for the original behavior now fails. That's okay: we intentionally changed the behavior that test asserted, making it obsolete. When tests become obsolete, it's appropriate to delete them. However, rather than deleting it, let's skip it for now as we might need some of that code later when testing the success path:

```
func testCallsGivenGroupingFunction() throws {
    try XCTSkipIf(true, "skipping this for now, keeping it to
    reuse part of the code later on")
    // ...
}
```

Skipping tests is better than commenting them. For each skipped test, you'll get an entry in the Xcode Test navigator as well as an inline notice. A commented test goes under the radar instead. Commented code tends to be forgotten and rot in the codebase; a skipped test is harder to miss.

Figures 7-1 and 7-2 show how Xcode shows a skipped test inline and in the Test navigator.

Figure 7-1. *How Xcode reports skipped tests inline in the code editor*

Figure 7-2. *How Xcode reports skipped tests in the Test navigator*

Our change to the ViewModel init made it ignore both menu and menuGrouping parameters. Usually, I'd encourage you to remove unused code once you are in the green state as part of the refactor step. In this case, we can expect to use that code as we move forward in the implementation, so we're better off keeping them.

We can use the green test as a safety guard to refactor MenuList. ViewModel to conform to ObservableObject. If during the refactor one of our changes breaks the behavior, the test will tell us.

Let's make MenuList.ViewModel conform to ObservableObject and wrap sections in @Published:

```
// MenuList.ViewModel.swift
import Combine

extension MenuList {

    class ViewModel: ObservableObject {

        @Published private(set) var sections: [MenuSection]
```

```
    init(
        menu: [MenuItem],
        menuGrouping: @escaping ([MenuItem]) ->
        [MenuSection] = groupMenuByCategory
    ) {
        self.sections = menuGrouping([])
    }
  }
}
```

There are a few things to notice in this change. First of all, we had to import Combine because it's this framework that defines the ObservableObject protocol and the @Published property wrapper.

MenuList.ViewModel had to become a class because ObservableObject requires the types conforming to it to be classes.

The sections property had to change from let to var. That's a requirement for being wrapped with @Published. It makes sense: published values can change over time.

Finally, to make sure that only the code internal to MenuList.ViewModel can change the sections, its access level is now private(set): consumers will be able to read it but not update it.

After these changes, the tests still pass. The refactor was successful.

Now that we configured MenuList.ViewModel to be an ObservableObject with a @Published property, it's time to start publishing values through it. For that, we have two tests left to write: one for the happy path, when the request succeeds, and another for the failure path, when the backend returns an error.

I usually recommend tackling the failure scenarios first to avoid neglecting error handling, because it's tempting to move to the next feature as soon as you finish implementing the happy path. In this case, however, the happy path looks similar to the fetching start behavior, which we

104

already implemented: from an empty array to one with elements. Starting from there has a lower entry threshold, it's a smaller step forward to take:

```
// MenuList.ViewModelTests.swift
// ...
func testWhenFecthingSucceedsPublishesSectionsBuiltFromReceived
MenuAndGivenGroupingClosure() {
    // Arrange the ViewModel and its data source

    // Act on the ViewModel to trigger the update

    // Assert the expected behavior
}
```

Writing this test's structure brings up two questions:

- How can we simulate a successful fetching when we don't have a real network component to use as the data source?

- The expected behavior is that the @Published sections update; how can we test @Published values?

Let's focus on simulating receiving a value in the menu fetching first.

The Dependency Inversion Principle

To simulate receiving a value or an error when fetching the menu, we need an object that fetches the menu in the first place. Eventually, that will be the networking component, but we haven't built it yet. Because we're working on the UI side of the fetching behavior, building the network component would be too big of a detour; it would slow down our feedback cycle. To solve this chicken-and-egg problem, we need to take a step back and look at our design.

Instead of expecting a concrete type for the menu fetching in `MenuList.ViewModel`, we can define an abstraction and interact with it. The Swift way to do this is by using a `protocol`:

```
// MenuFetching.swift
import Combine

protocol MenuFetching {

    func fetchMenu() -> AnyPublisher<[MenuItem], Error>
}
```

The `fetchMenu` method returns an `AnyPublisher` with a `[MenuItem]` as its output. Combine defines `AnyPublisher` as a specialized `Publisher` meant only for consumption; you cannot `send` new values from it, only subscribe.

In *Agile Software Development: Principles, Patterns, and Practices*, Robert C. Martin calls this technique of defining an abstraction between components **Dependency Inversion Principle**, DIP for short.

DIP states that "High-level modules should not depend on low-level modules. Both should depend on abstractions." That is, `MenuList.ViewModel` should not depend on the object performing the network request but on an abstraction of the menu fetching operation. In our context, this means defining a `protocol` to represent the abstraction, `MenuFetching`, and have `MenuList.ViewModel` use it as the type it expects for its menu fetching component.

The term "inversion" refers to the change from the dependency relationship used in the Object-Oriented Design methods at the time the principle was introduced, where high-level modules depended on low-level ones. In the traditional model, a change in a low-level module would require a change in the high-level module too, because of their direct dependency. "This predicament is absurd!" Martin exclaims. "It is the high-level, policy-setting modules that ought to be influencing the low-level, detailed modules. The modules that contain the high-level business rules should take precedence over, and be independent of, the modules that contain the implementation details."

Applying Dependency Inversion has positive practical consequences in both the production and test code. In the production code, we can build a simple object conforming to `MenuFetching` for the ViewModel to use while we wait for the networking component to be ready. In the tests, we can create an object conforming to the protocol and simulate the fetch operation's different results with it to verify how the ViewModel behaves. Objects created to simulate production ones during testing are called *Test Doubles*, and we'll learn about them in the next chapter.

DEPENDENCY INVERSION VS. DEPENDENCY INJECTION

Though they have similar names, it's crucial not to confuse dependency *inversion* with *injection.*

The Dependency Inversion Principle states you should define abstractions for the components to depend upon so that changes in a low-level component won't affect the higher-level ones using it.

Dependency Injection happens when you make your objects require instances of the other components in the system they need to interact with rather than creating them internally.

Both DIP and DI make your software design more flexible but in subtly different ways: one refers to how objects should interact and the other to how objects should be built.

Decouple the ViewModel from the Data Fetching with DIP

We've seen that to decouple the ViewModel from the data fetching implementation details, we need to make it depend on the `MenuFetching` abstraction. Let's implement this change starting from the production code.

You might be asking: "Why aren't we starting with a test?" When practicing TDD, you're optimizing for fast feedback cycles. As we've seen in Chapter 3, the compiler is also part of the TDD workflow. In this instance, starting from a change in the production code rather than the tests gives us faster feedback because the compiler will point out all the code that needs to be updated:

```swift
// MenuList.ViewModel.swift
extension MenuList {

    class ViewModel: ObservableObject {

        @Published private(set) var sections: [MenuSection]

        init(
            menuFetching: MenuFetching,
            menuGrouping: @escaping ([MenuItem]) ->
            [MenuSection] = groupMenuByCategory
        ) {
            self.sections = menuGrouping([])
        }
    }
}
```

If you try to build the app and its test target with the `Shift Cmd U` keyboard shortcut, you'll see one compiler error in `AlbertosApp.swift`:

```
MenuList(viewModel: .init(menu: menu))
  // Compiler says:
  // - Extra argument 'menu' in call
  // - Missing argument for parameter 'menuFetching' in call
```

The compiler tells us that AlbertosApp needs to provide an instance of a type conforming to MenuFetching to the MenuList.ViewModel init.

That means that, for the app to compile, we need to update the ViewModel call site, giving it a MenuFetching instance. To do so, we need first to create an object conforming to MenuFetching.

As we discussed, instead of providing a "real" implementation, we should quickly build a placeholder so we can stay focused on dynamically updating the UI. Because the final implementation will also conform to MenuFetching, we'll be able to swap it in once ready, and MenuList. ViewModel will be none the wiser:

```
// MenuFetchingPlaceholder.swift
import Combine
import Foundation

class MenuFetchingPlaceholder: MenuFetching {

    func fetchMenu() -> AnyPublisher<[MenuItem], Error> {
        return Future { $0(.success(menu)) }
            // Use a delay to simulate async fetch
            .delay(for: 0.5, scheduler: RunLoop.main)
            .eraseToAnyPublisher()
    }
}
```

Future is a Combine convenience type to create "a publisher that eventually produces a single value and then finishes or fails." Future { $0(.success(menu)) } creates a Publisher that emits menu and then finishes. menu is the hardcoded global MenuItem array we defined in Chapter 4, as part of our first iteration on the app.

We now have all we need to update the MenuList.ViewModel call site in the source code:

```
// AlbertosApp.swift
@main
struct AlbertosApp: App {
    var body: some Scene {
        WindowGroup {
            NavigationView {
                MenuList(
                    viewModel: .init(
                        menuFetching: MenuFetchingPlaceholder()
                    )
                )
                .navigationTitle("Alberto's 🍝")
            }
        }
    }
}
```

If you run Shift Cmd U again, you'll see the build still fails, but this time in the test target. We didn't see those errors before because Xcode only tries to build the test target if the production one builds first.

These new compiler errors are also due to the MenuList.ViewModel init calls not using MenuFetching. We can fix them in the same manner as the production code: by using MenuFetchingPlaceholder.

From this:

```
let viewModel = MenuList.ViewModel(menu: [.fixture()])
```

To this:

```
let viewModel = MenuList.ViewModel(
    menuFetching: MenuFetchingPlaceholder()
)
```

The tests now build, and if you run them, you'll see they pass too.

We have the abstraction layer in place, and we're back in the green state: let's move forward and implement the test for how the ViewModel updates its sections when the menu fetch succeeds.

How to Test Async Updates of `@Published` Properties

We want to verify that, when the menu fetch succeeds, the `@Published` value updates with the sections generated from the received `[MenuItem]`.

When you wrap a property with `@Published`, the compiler creates a `Publisher` for it. This `Publisher` will publish a new value every time the property updates, and you can access it using the $ prefix. Therefore, to test how a `@Published` property updates means to test the behavior of its `Publisher`.

`Publishers` transmit a sequence of values over time; they behave asynchronously. As we discussed in Chapter 2, XCTest's primary tool for testing asynchronous code is `XCTExpectation`.

Here's the test:

```
// MenuList.ViewModelTests.swift
// ...
class MenuListViewModelTests: XCTestCase {

    var cancellables = Set<AnyCancellable>()

    // ...

    func testWhenFecthingSucceedsPublishesSectionsBuiltFrom
    ReceivedMenuAndGivenGroupingClosure() {
        var receivedMenu: [MenuItem]?
        let expectedSections = [MenuSection.fixture()]
```

```
    let spyClosure: ([MenuItem]) -> [MenuSection] = { items in
        receivedMenu = items
        return expectedSections
    }

    let viewModel = MenuList.ViewModel(menuFetching:
    MenuFetchingPlaceholder(), menuGrouping: spyClosure)

    let expectation = XCTestExpectation(
        description: "Publishes sections built from
        received menu and given grouping closure"
    )

    viewModel
        .$sections
        .dropFirst()
        .sink { value in
            // Ensure the grouping closure is called with
            // the received menu
            XCTAssertEqual(receivedMenu, menu)
            // Ensure the published value is the result of
            // the grouping closure
            XCTAssertEqual(value, expectedSections)
            expectation.fulfill()
        }
        .store(in: &cancellables)

    wait(for: [expectation], timeout: 1)
    }

    // ...
}
```

Let's unpack what's happening. The test

1. Sets up the spy closure as we did in the static version of the test.

2. Instantiates `MenuList.ViewModel` passing it a `MenuFetchingPlaceholder` instance. This allows us to simulate the successful menu fetching scenario.

3. Defines an `XCTestExpectation` to test the asynchronous publishing behavior.

4. Accesses the `Publisher` from the `@Published` `sections` property of the ViewModel using the `$` prefix.

5. Calls `dropFirst()` to skip the first received value. The first published value is the default one set in the property definition. By ignoring it, we can read the next one that comes and see if it matches our expectation without tracking the multiple values the `Publisher` emits, simplifying the test setup.

6. Attaches a subscriber closure to the `Publisher` stream using `.sink`.

7. In the observer, asserts that `value` is the `menu` returned by `MenuFetchingPlaceholder` and was built using the given grouping closure and then fulfills the `expectation`.

8. Stores the `AnyCancellable` returned by the `sink` call into a `Set`. We need to do this to have a memory reference to the stream of events, or its allocated memory will be released before it gets a chance to emit values.

The test is failing with "Asynchronous wait failed: Exceeded timeout of 1 seconds, with unfulfilled expectations: 'Publishes sections build from received menu and given grouping closure.'" To make it pass, let's add the code to subscribe to menu fetcher `Publisher` and update our sections when a new value arrives:

```
// MenuList.ViewModel.swift
// ...
init(
    menuFetching: MenuFetching,
    menuGrouping: @escaping ([MenuItem]) -> [MenuSection] =
    groupMenuByCategory
) {
    sections = []
    menuFetching
        .fetchMenu()
        .sink(
            receiveCompletion: { _ in },
            receiveValue: { [weak self] value in
                self?.sections = menuGrouping(value)
            }
        )
        .store(in: &cancellables)
}
```

The test now passes. We only have one step left: make `MenuList` observe the ViewModel so SwiftUI can update it when the data becomes available. That's as easy as wrapping the `viewModel` property in `@ObservedObject`:

```
@ObservedObject var viewModel: ViewModel
```

If you run the app now, you'll see it behaves just as before, only with the little difference that the menu appears on-screen a moment's delay – 0.5 seconds to be precise, the value we set in `MenuFetchingPlaceholder`.

Something noticeably missing from the current flow is the loading state management. There's no indication the app is loading data; customers stare at an empty screen until, suddenly, the menu appears.

Proper handling of the loading state is a must-have for every app, but, in the interest of moving forward with learning new concepts, we won't be implementing it here. Feel free to work on it as an exercise.

A simple implementation could be using the content of the menu array as a proxy for the loading state: if it's empty, then the app must be waiting for a response. A more elegant and robust solution would be to represent all the view's possible states (not asked, loading, loaded, failed to load) in an enum. Have a look at `RemoteData` for a sample of this approach.

Mystery Guest

There's something suboptimal about the test we just wrote. A reader with less context than us may not immediately understand why we assert that the received menu is equal to a global value called `menu`. This value is a mysterious guest in the test; it's not immediately clear where it came from or why it's there.

When the cause-effect relationship between the inputs and outputs of a test is not straightforward, understanding the test becomes harder and, if the test fails, so does finding the source of the failure. You should avoid having Mystery Guests in your test and always strive to give a reader all the information they need to understand the code. We'll see how to remove this particular Mystery Guest instance shortly.

In this chapter, we applied *Partition Problem and Solve Sequentially* to the task of fetching the menu from a remote API and loading it on-screen. We chose to start with the logic to update the UI when the menu data becomes available. Our implementation is rough and incomplete, but it works nevertheless. It's a solid foundation on which to keep building.

We evolved our initial static ViewModel into one that fetches its data from an asynchronous source, streaming the change to its consumer using one of the SwiftUI and Combine native data flow mechanisms. Leveraging the frameworks vastly simplified our job as we had to focus only on asking and transforming the data while they handled keeping the view up-to-date.

We got to a working implementation without real data fetching from the network by applying the *Dependency Inversion Principle* to define an abstraction layer between ViewModel and networking. By having a placeholder for the networking part behind the abstraction layer, we were able to implement the desired `MenuList.ViewModel` behavior for when the API returns a successful value test first.

We still need to tackle the failure scenario. And what about removing the Mystery Guest? That's what we'll work on in the next chapter.

Practice Time

The test for the `@Published` property we wrote has the implicit assumption that there's going to be only one value published after the default initial one. That's the behavior we expect from a network request to a remote REST API: make an HTTP call that can either succeed or fail.

A `Publisher`, on the other hand, can emit *many* values over time.

To learn how to work with the multiple values a `Publisher` sends, try rewriting the test without using `dropFirst()` and verify that the first value received is an empty array and the second matches the menu transformation expectation.

Key Takeaways

- **SwiftUI and Combine make updating a view as new data comes out easy with `ObservableObject`, `@Published`, and `@ObservedObject`**. Use these tools to have the frameworks automatically update your view every time new values are published.

- **Apply the Dependency Inversion Principle to decouple ViewModels from the implementation details of data fetching using an abstraction layer**. You can define a `protocol` for the ViewModel to request instead of a concrete type.

- **An abstraction layer allows you to provide placeholder implementations for components that are not ready yet**. You can focus on building one piece at a time without going off a tangent to build its dependencies first.

- **You can test async updates of `@Published` properties using `sink` and `XCTestExpectation`**. By subscribing to the `Publisher` associated with a `@Published` property, you can test how it changes over time.

- **Use `XCTSkipIf(_:, _:)` instead of commenting test code you are not ready to delete yet**. This API generates an entry in the test report, making it harder to forget about the code and pollute the codebase with out-of-date comments.

CHAPTER 8

Testing Code Based on Indirect Inputs

How do you test behavior that depends on indirect inputs in isolation?

By building a test-specific replacement for the dependency, which you can use to control the indirect inputs it provides to the system under test.

We're in the middle of building the UI component of the new menu fetching from a remote API functionality. We started from the UI to have an *Earliest Testable* version of the dynamic update, but that means we don't have the real networking component yet.

In the previous chapter, we applied the *Dependency Injection Principle* and defined an abstraction for the ViewModel to depend upon, MenuFetching, which lets us use a placeholder implementation for the networking object and stay focused on the current task. That allowed us to write tests to drive making MenuList.ViewModel update the view once it receives the menu data, but those tests are incomplete: we haven't tested error handling, and there's a Mystery Guest in the successful fetching test.

The challenge in testing how MenuList.ViewModel behaves is that it depends on the indirect input MenuFetching feeds it. So far, we tested components with methods expecting an input and returning an output, but MenuList.ViewModel's input comes from the return value it gets when calling MenuFetching fetchMenu() internally.

In this chapter, we'll learn how to work around this constraint using a *Stub Test Double* to get granular control over the indirect input that `MenuFetching` sends `MenuList.ViewModel`.

The Stub Test Double

In the previous chapter, we wrote the following test for the successful menu fetching scenario:

```
// MenuList.ViewModelTests.swift
func testWhenFecthingSucceedsPublishesSectionsBuiltFromReceived
MenuAndGivenGroupingClosure() {
    var receivedMenu: [MenuItem]?
    let expectedSections = [MenuSection.fixture()]
    let spyClosure: ([MenuItem]) -> [MenuSection] = { items in
        receivedMenu = items
        return expectedSections
    }

    let viewModel = MenuList.ViewModel(menuFetching:
    MenuFetchingPlaceholder(), menuGrouping: spyClosure)

    let expectation = XCTestExpectation(
        description: "Publishes sections built from received
        menu and given grouping closure"
    )

    viewModel
        .$sections
        .dropFirst()
        .sink { value in
            // Ensure the grouping closure is called with the
            // received menu
```

```
    XCTAssertEqual(receivedMenu, menu)
    // Ensure the published value is the result of the
    // grouping closure
    XCTAssertEqual(value, expectedSections)
    expectation.fulfill()
}
.store(in: &cancellables)

  wait(for: [expectation], timeout: 1)
}
```

The test uses the global menu constant to assert the ViewModel calls its grouping closure correctly. menu is a *Mystery Guest*: unless you recently looked at the MenuFetchingPlaceholder implementation, you won't know that's the value it returns.

Tests that are hard to understand are a liability: when they fail, it will take longer to figure out why and, consequently, to fix them. A developer who's in a rush or doesn't appreciate the value of testing might end up commenting the test "to fix later," but we all know later is never.

How can we make the relationship between the indirect input and the resulting behavior clear? Is there a way to configure the indirect input in the Arrange phase in the same straightforward way we've done for the direct inputs of the tests we've seen so far? Yes, there is.

Because MenuList.ViewModel depends on an abstraction instead of a concrete type, nothing stops us from building another MenuFetching implementation where we can configure the indirect input it delivers and use it in the tests.

In *xUnit Test Patterns*, Gerard Meszaros calls this kind of "test-specific equivalent" of a dependency of the system under test a *Test Double*.

There are different kinds of Test Doubles we can use depending on the role the dependency plays in the behavior being tested. The one we're about to build is a *Stub*.

A Stub is a Test Double that provides control over the indirect inputs of the system under test:

```swift
// MenuFetchingStub.swift
@testable import Albertos
import Combine
import Foundation

class MenuFetchingStub: MenuFetching {

    let result: Result<[MenuItem], Error>

    init(returning result: Result<[MenuItem], Error>) {
        self.result = result
    }

    func fetchMenu() -> AnyPublisher<[MenuItem], Error> {
        return result.publisher
            // Use a delay to simulate the real world async behavior
            .delay(for: 0.1, scheduler: RunLoop.main)
            .eraseToAnyPublisher()
    }
}
```

How a Stub works depends on the kind of dependency it replaces, but the guiding rule is to always provide a way to configure the desired input and use it in the Stub's implementation.

In this case, we initialize the Stub with a Result for the response and then convert it to an AnyPublisher to use as the return value of fetchMenu().

Also, notice the delay to simulate the asynchronous behavior. Sometimes, it's useful to remove asynchronous behavior from the tests by providing them with Test Doubles that immediately return the desired value. In this case, however, the asynchronous behavior is precisely what we're trying to implement. Removing the delay would separate the test from the real behavior and might result in a false positive.

We can now expel the mysterious menu guest by replacing MenuFetchingPlaceholder with MenuFetchingStub:

```
func testWhenFecthingSucceedsPublishesSectionsBuiltFromReceived
MenuAndGivenGroupingClosure() {
    var receivedMenu: [MenuItem]?
    let expectedSections = [MenuSection.fixture()]
    let spyClosure: ([MenuItem]) -> [MenuSection] = { items in
        receivedMenu = items
        return expectedSections
    }

    let expectedMenu = [MenuItem.fixture()]
    let menuFetchingStub = MenuFetchingStub(returning:
    .success(expectedMenu))

    let viewModel = MenuList.ViewModel(menuFetching:
    menuFetchingStub, menuGrouping: spyClosure)
    let expectation = XCTestExpectation(
        description: "Publishes sections built from received
        menu and given grouping closure"
    )

    viewModel
        .$sections
        .dropFirst()
        .sink { value in
            // Ensure the grouping closure is called with the
            // received menu
            XCTAssertEqual(receivedMenu, expectedMenu)
            // Ensure the published value is the result of the
            // grouping closure
```

```
        XCTAssertEqual(value, expectedSections)
        expectation.fulfill()
    }
    .store(in: &cancellables)

  wait(for: [expectation], timeout: 1)
}
```

The test still passes. As far as MenuList.ViewModel is concerned, nothing has changed. The ViewModel doesn't know or care which concrete MenuFetching implementation we give to it, whether it's a placeholder, a Test Double, or the real one.

We now have a clear cause-effect relationship between the SUT indirect input and its output. Let's move to the last but equally important test in our list: the one for error handling.

Make Error Handling Explicit with Result

Right now, the sections property type is [MenuSection], but MenuFetching can also emit an error, and the view needs to be able to show it.

To handle both scenarios, we can use the Result type. Sections can become a Result<[MenuSection], Error>, and we can update MenuList to render differently depending on whether it's a success or failure.

The beauty of using an enum like Result is that it makes the mutually exclusive relationship between the success and failure cases explicit at the type system level. The view can either be in the success or failure state, and the Result instance can either be a .success or .failure case.

Let's make this change using compiler errors as a fast-feedback mechanism:

```
// MenuList.ViewModel.swift
// ...
class ViewModel: ObservedObject {
```

```swift
@Published private var sections: Result<[MenuSection],
Error> = .success([])

init(
    menuFetching: MenuFetching,
    menuGrouping: @escaping ([MenuItem]) -> [MenuSection] =
    groupMenuByCategory
) {
menuFetching
    .fetchMenu()
    .sink(
        receiveCompletion: { _ in },
        receiveValue: { [weak self] value in
            self?.sections = .success(menuGrouping(value))
        }
    )
    .store(in: &cancellables)
```

After we update MenuList.ViewModel, its view fails to build because of the type change:

```swift
// MenuList.swift
// ...
var body: some View {
    List {
        ForEach(viewModel.sections) { section in
            // Compiler says: Cannot convert value of type
            // 'Result<[MenuSection], Error>'
            // to expected argument type 'Range<Int>'
            //
            // Plus more errors in the following access to
            // sections...
```

We need to update MenuList to handle both success and failure cases of the Result type:

```swift
// MenuList.swift
// ...
var body: some View {
    switch viewModel.sections {
    case .success(let sections):
        List {
            ForEach(sections) { section in
                Section(header: Text(section.category)) {
                    ForEach(section.items) { item in
                        MenuRow(viewModel: .init(item: item))
                    }
                }
            }
        }
    case .failure(let error):
        Text("An error occurred:")
        Text(error.localizedDescription).italic()
    }
}
```

With MenuList updated, the source code builds successfully, but the tests don't. As we already discussed in the previous chapter, we see this failure only now because Xcode doesn't build the test targets unless their production target builds first.

The compiler highlights the code we need to update in the tests, with failures like:

```
// MenuList.ViewModelTests.swift
// ...
XCTAssertTrue(viewModel.sections.isEmpty)
    // Compiler says: Cannot convert value of type
    // 'Result<[MenuSection], Error>'
    // to expected argument type 'Range<Int>'
```

Let's update the test for the default value behavior first:

```
// MenuList.ViewModelTests.swift
// ...
func testWhenFetchingStartsPublishesEmptyMenu() throws {
    let viewModel = MenuList.ViewModel(menuFetching:
    MenuFetchingStub(returning: .success([.fixture()])))

    let sections = try viewModel.sections.get()

    XCTAssertTrue(sections.isEmpty)
}
```

.get() is a handy Result method that will return the associated value of a successful instance and throw otherwise.

Another option to ensure that our Result value is a success is to use a guard case statement. Here it is in action in the test for the successful scenario:

```
// MenuList.ViewModelTests.swift
// ...
func testWhenFecthingSucceedsPublishesSectionsBuiltFromReceived
MenuAndGivenGroupingClosure() {
    // ...
    viewModel
        .$sections
        .dropFirst()
```

```
    .sink { value in
        guard case .success(let sections) = value else {
            return XCTFail("Expected a successful Result,
            got: \(value)")
        }

        // Ensure the grouping closure is called with the
        // received menu
        XCTAssertEqual(receivedMenu, expectedMenu)
        // Ensure the published value is the result of the
        // grouping closure
        XCTAssertEqual(sections, expectedSections)
        expectation.fulfill()
    }
    .store(in: &cancellables)
// ...
}
```

The code now compiles, and the tests are still green. We can proceed with the test for the failure behavior at last. We've done all of the learning on how to write tests for @Published values and Result type already; now it's only a matter of using a different state setup and expectation.

To provide our SUT with a failure from MenuFetching, we need to initialize MenuFetchingStub with a failure value. What should we use as the error?

The sections type uses the generic Error in its definition, but we need a concrete one in the test. We can define a dedicated error type for the tests:

```
// TestError.swift
struct TestError: Equatable, Error {
    let id: Int
}
```

By conforming `TestError` to `Equatable`, we can use it with
`XCTAssertEqual` and make testing straightforward.

Let's configure the Stub to return a known test error and ensure our
code passes it through to `sections`:

```swift
func testWhenFetchingFailsPublishesAnError() {
    let expectedError = TestError(id: 123)
    let menuFetchingStub = MenuFetchingStub(returning:
    .failure(expectedError))

    let viewModel = MenuList.ViewModel(menuFetching:
    menuFetchingStub, menuGrouping: { _ in [] })

    let expectation = XCTestExpectation(description: "Publishes
    an error")

    viewModel
        .$sections
        .dropFirst()
        .sink { value in
            guard case .failure(let error) = value else {
                return XCTFail("Expected a failing Result,
                got: \(value)")
            }

            XCTAssertEqual(error as? TestError, expectedError)
            expectation.fulfill()
        }
        .store(in: &cancellables)

    wait(for: [expectation], timeout: 1)
}
```

The test fails with a timeout. To make it pass, we need to handle the possible .failure published by MenuFetching in the ViewModel:

```
// MenuList.ViewModel.swift
// ...
menuFetching
    .fetchMenu()
    .sink(
        receiveCompletion: { [weak self] completion in
            guard case .failure(let error) = completion else
            { return }
            self?.sections = .failure(error)
        },
        receiveValue: { [weak self] value in
            self?.sections = .success(menuGrouping(value))
        }
    )
    .store(in: &cancellables)
```

Now that we are in the green state and the functionality is complete, it's time to ask the question of whether we can improve the code we've written so far.

A nice touch would be to extract the transformation from [MenuItem] to [MenuSection] into a dedicated step:

```
menuFetching
    .fetchMenu()
    .map(menuGrouping)
    .sink(
        receiveCompletion: { [weak self] completion in
            guard case .failure(let error) = completion else
            { return }
```

```
        self?.sections = .failure(error)
    },
    receiveValue: { [weak self] value in
        self?.sections = .success(value)
    }
)
.store(in: &cancellables)
```

This separation between input manipulation and value assignment to the @Published property makes the data flow clearer.

The *Dependency Inversion Principle* states that higher-level components should not depend on lower-level ones but on abstractions. Between this and the previous chapter, we've seen the practical benefits of applying this principle.

We've built a fully functioning dynamically updating UI to show the menu list fetched from a remote API even though we don't have the networking component yet. We're confident our implementation works now and will work when we plug the real API fetching into it because the tests that guided writing it used a *Stub* to simulate the possible inputs a MenuFetching-conforming type can produce.

Now that the code closer to the view layer is in place, the next step is to move one layer beneath and translate JSON data into MenuItems.

Practice Time

You decide to make the menu UX more resilient by adding a retry functionality. The failure view should have a button that makes the ViewModel start a new menu fetch.

How can you test this new behavior?

Hint   A possible way to do it is to make the Stub publish different values, such as a failure first and then a success, and write a test that exercises the retry method and verifies the sequence of published values.

Key Takeaways

- **Applying the Dependency Inversion Principle allows you to write tests using Test Doubles**. Test Doubles are "test-specific equivalents" of the SUT's dependency that you can use to keep tests isolated and simulate different behaviors.

- **Replace a dependency with a Stub to control the indirect inputs it provides to the SUT**. With a Stub, you can test many different indirect input scenarios, always making the causal relationship between input and output explicit.

- **Use enums to describe the mutually exclusive states a SwiftUI view can be in**. For example, use Result to represent content generated by an operation that either succeeded or failed.

CHAPTER 9

Testing JSON Decoding

How do you use tests to drive writing logic to decode JSON data into a model object?

By feeding the tests a predefined JSON input and verify the decoding produces a value matching it.

Swift's Decodable protocol offers a type-safe way to describe how to transform Data, such as a JSON in the body of an HTTP response, into an object or value type. With Decodable doing most of the heavy lifting, is it worth using tests to drive the implementation of JSON decoding logic?

When the JSON object has keys and values with names and types that map directly to Swift, there is no real logic you need to write to decode it. In such a case, you may feel comfortable writing the source code directly, without the help of a unit test. If the JSON object is elaborate or if you want to decode it into a Swift type with a different structure, then a test will help you along the way.

Choosing whether to deploy TDD to implement JSON decoding logic is a matter of tradeoffs. Is the extra time you're spending writing the test worth the feedback it gives you? Once the test is in place, will it guard against regression that may otherwise go unnoticed?

To answer those questions, you first need to know how to write this kind of tests. In this chapter, we'll explore two different techniques to write

© Gio Lodi 2021
G. Lodi, *Test-Driven Development in Swift*, https://doi.org/10.1007/978-1-4842-7002-8_9

tests for JSON decoding and reflect further on the return on investment of applying TDD to this part of the app's implementation.

We're moving along steadily in making our app fetch the menu from a remote API. In the previous chapters, we built the view part of this new functionality. It's now time to take one step further down the stack, coding the conversion from the raw `Data` a network request would return into the `MenuItem` domain model.

Swift provides a convenient way to decode `Data` into a different type via the `Decodable` protocol. Our job is to conform `MenuItem` to it and verify the decoding is successful.

As part of your application development agreement with Alberto, you're also building his backend service. You chose to use a REST API that returns a JSON menu in the following form:[1]

```
[
    {
        "name": "spaghetti carbonara",
        "category": "pasta",
        "spicy": false
    },
    {
        "name": "penne all'arrabbiata",
        "category": "pasta",
        "spicy": true
    }
]
```

How do we go from that JSON to a `MenuItem` using TDD? As always, we start with a test. In this instance, we'll write a test for the decoding behavior.

The question to ask when writing a test is how to verify if the desired behavior occurred. Our desired behavior is a successful JSON decoding. To verify it, we need to devise a test asserting that, given a particular JSON input, the decoded Swift object has matching properties:

```swift
// MenuItemTests.swift
@testable import Albertos
import XCTest

class MenuItemTests: XCTestCase {

    func testWhenDecodedFromJSONDataHasAllTheInputProperties() {
        // arrange the JSON Data input

        // act by decoding a MenuItem instance from the Data

        // assert the MenuItem matches the input
    }
}
```

If the input is:

```
{
    "name": "a name",
    "category": "a category",
    "spicy": true
}
```

then our expectations shall be:

```swift
// MenuItemTests.swift
// ...
func testWhenDecodedFromJSONDataHasAllTheInputProperties() {
    // arrange the JSON Data input

    // act by decoding a MenuItem instance from the Data

    XCTAssertEqual(item.name, "a name")
    XCTAssertEqual(item.category, "a category")
    XCTAssertEqual(item.spicy, true)
}
```

Swift's JSONDecoder is the type to use to get the item instance from the input JSON Data:

```swift
// MenuItemTests.swift
// ...
func testWhenDecodedFromJSONDataHasAllTheInputProperties()
throws {
    // arrange the JSON Data input

    let item = try JSONDecoder()
        .decode(MenuItem.self, from: data)

    XCTAssertEqual(item.name, "a name")
    XCTAssertEqual(item.category, "a category")
    XCTAssertEqual(item.spicy, true)
}
```

How can we arrange the JSON input for the test? Let's see two different approaches.

Option 1: Inline Strings

One option to generate the JSON input is to define it as a `String` inline in
the test and then convert it into `Data`:

```
// MenuItemTests.swift
// ...
func testWhenDecodedFromJSONDataHasAllTheInputProperties()
throws {
    let json = #"{ "name": "a name", "category": "a category",
    "spicy": true }"#
    let data = try XCTUnwrap(json.data(using: .utf8))
        // Compiler says: Instance method 'decode(_:from:)'
        // requires
        // that 'MenuItem' conform to 'Decodable'

    let item = try JSONDecoder().decode(MenuItem.self, from:
    data)

    XCTAssertEqual(item.name, "a name")
    XCTAssertEqual(item.category, "a category")
    XCTAssertEqual(item.spicy, true)
}
```

The compiler points out that our `MenuItem` does not conform to
`Decodable`. Let's satisfy this condition:

```
// MenuItem.swift
struct MenuItem {
    // ...
}

// ...

extension MenuItem: Decodable {}
```

The test builds now. It also passes already because the names of the properties in `MenuItem` match the names of the keys in the JSON input, so the compiler takes care of all the decoding for us.

The fact that the test passed when the only change we made was to conform to a `protocol` without any extra code raises a question: are we testing our code's behavior or that of `Decodable`?

As mentioned in this chapter's introduction, there are instances in which using a test to drive the JSON decoding implementation may be an unnecessary overhead. We're learning how to write this kind of tests to discern when they are useful and when they aren't. Let's look at another option for the Arrange phase and then discuss when using TDD for JSON decoding is appropriate.

Option 2: JSON Files

Another option to provide the input for our test is to have JSON files holding the input values.

To add a JSON file to your test target

1. Select the test target folder in the project navigator.

2. Right-click it and click "New File..." or press `Cmd  N`.

3. Select the Other ➤ Empty file and then click "Next" or press `Enter`.

Figure 9-1 shows the Empty file option from the Xcode "New File..." dialog.

Choose a template for your new file:

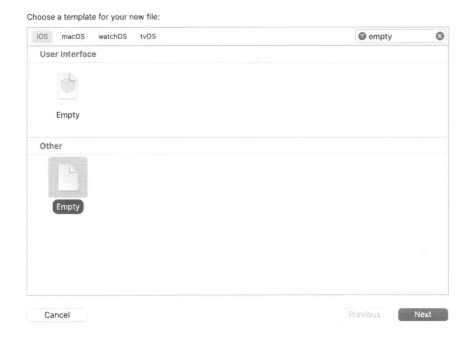

Figure 9-1. *The Xcode New File... dialog, filtered to show only empty file templates*

4. Add the .json extension to the file name and select "Create" or press Enter.

Figure 9-2 shows the final dialog in the "New File..." sequence, where you can choose the name, location, and target for the file.

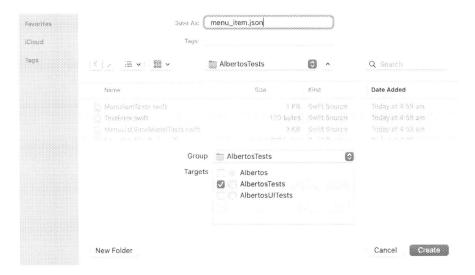

Figure 9-2. *The Xcode dialog to name and add a new file to the file system and project targets*

5.   Populate the file with the JSON for the menu item:

```
// menu_item.json
{
    "name": "a name",
    "category": "a category",
    "spicy": true
}
```

Alternatively, you can create the JSON file with your favorite text editor and save it into the test target folder. From Xcode, you can then right-click the test target folder and select "Add Files To '`<test target name>`'..." or press `Cmd Alt A` to reveal a file navigator where to select your JSON file.

Once the file is part of the project, you can load it in the tests like this:

```
// MenuItemTests.swift
// ...
func testDecodesFromJSONData() throws {
```

```
let url = try XCTUnwrap(
    Bundle(for: type(of: self)).url(forResource:
    "menu_item", withExtension: "json")
)
let data = try Data(contentsOf: url)

let item = try JSONDecoder().decode(MenuItem.self, from:
data)

XCTAssertEqual(item.name, "a name")
XCTAssertEqual(item.category, "a category")
XCTAssertEqual(item.spicy, true)
}
```

If you haven't removed the source changes we wrote in the previous example, this test will immediately pass.

We can make the test code tidier by extracting the file-reading logic into a helper function. This is useful to do if you have more than a couple of tests for model decoding:

```
// XCTestCase+JSON.swift
import XCTest

extension XCTestCase {

    func dataFromJSONFileNamed(_ name: String) throws -> Data {
        let url = try XCTUnwrap(
            Bundle(for: type(of: self)).url(forResource: name,
            withExtension: "json")
        )
        return try Data(contentsOf: url)
    }
}
```

```swift
// MenuItemTests.swift
// ...
func testDecodesFromJSONData() throws {
    let data = try dataFromJSONFileNamed("menu_item")

    let item = try JSONDecoder()
        .decode(MenuItem.self, from: data)

    XCTAssertEqual(item.name, "a name")
    XCTAssertEqual(item.category, "a category")
    XCTAssertEqual(item.spicy, true)
}
```

Which Option to Choose?

The advantage of using inline strings is that you can keep the input values close to the expectation they support. With the JSON file option, it's unclear where "a name," "a category," and true come from, the only way to be sure is to check the JSON file as well.

On the other hand, using JSON files makes our tests tidier. As your input JSON grows in size, the inline string approach will result in longer and longer test methods, whereas tests loading the data from a file won't need more input setup code.

Using JSON files is also useful if you can automate generating them from your API, making sure the decoding is up to date without putting in place a full end-to-end integration test suite.

If you have input data that varies a lot, you'll end up with many JSON files, one for each variation. In this case, generating the input via string interpolation might be easier to maintain:

```swift
// MenuItem+JSONFixture.swift
@testable import Albertos
```

```
extension MenuItem {

    static func jsonFixture(
        name: String = "a name",
        category: String = "a category",
        spicy: Bool = false
    ) -> String {
        return """
{
    "name": "\(name)",
    "category": "\(category)",
    "spicy": \(spicy)
}
"""
    }
}

// MenuItemTests.swift
// ...
func testWhenDecodedFromJSONDataHasAllTheInputProperties()
throws {
    let json = MenuItem.jsonFixture(
        name: "a name",
        category: "a category",
        spicy: false
    )
    let data = try XCTUnwrap(json.data(using: .utf8))

    let item = try JSONDecoder().decode(MenuItem.self, from: data)

    XCTAssertEqual(item.name, "a name")
    XCTAssertEqual(item.category, "a category")
    XCTAssertEqual(item.spicy, false)
}
```

Which option to choose depends on your domain model. If your API has many entities, each rich with properties, then using files might make it easier to navigate your test suite.

Unless you are building an app against an existing API and already know what you're dealing with, I recommend starting with inline strings and optimizing your tests' understandability.

Now that we've explored the *how* of JSON decoding testing, let's take a step back and look at the *when*. When is TDD useful to implement JSON decoding?

Is Testing JSON Decoding Worth It?

It depends. Like everything else in software development, it's a matter of tradeoffs.

In the tests we wrote earlier, most of what we're testing is the behavior of Swift's `JSONDecoder`. That's code that we can't control, and, since it comes from the Swift standard library, it's safe to assume it works as advertised.

If all you need to decode JSON data coming from an API is adding `Decodable` to the list of protocols a type conforms to, then a test may not be worth it. If you still want to have a safeguard against the code breaking, you can write a simpler test, one that merely ensures the decoding doesn't throw an error:

```
func testWhenDecodingFromJSONDataDoesNotThrow() throws {
    let json = #"{ "name": "a name", "category": "a category",
        "spicy": true }"#
    let data = try XCTUnwrap(json.data(using: .utf8))

    XCTAssertNoThrow(try JSONDecoder().decode(MenuItem.self,
    from: data))
}
```

If you're doing something nontrivial in the decoding, then a test to make sure everything is working correctly is valuable.

For example, let's say the JSON comes with an object for the category instead of a plain string:

```
{
    "name": "tortellini alla panna",
    "category": {
        "name": "pasta",
        "id": 123
    },
    "spicy": false
}
```

To decode this JSON into our MenuItem object, we need some extra code on top of what the compiler synthesizes for us via Decodable:

Let's update our initial test with this input and see what happens:

```
// MenuItemTests.swift
// ...
func testWhenDecodedFromJSONDataHasAllTheInputProperties()
throws {
    let json = """
{
    "name": "a name",
    "category": {
        "name": "a category",
        "id": 123
    },
    "spicy": false
}
"""
```

```
    let data = try XCTUnwrap(json.data(using: .utf8))

    let item = try JSONDecoder()
        .decode(MenuItem.self, from: data)

    XCTAssertEqual(item.name, "a name")
    XCTAssertEqual(item.category, "a category")
    XCTAssertEqual(item.spicy, false)
}
```

The test fails with

```
typeMismatch(
    Swift.String,
    Swift.DecodingError.Context(
        codingPath: [
            CodingKeys(stringValue: "category", intValue: nil)
        ],
        debugDescription: "Expected to decode String but found
        a dictionary instead.", underlyingError: nil
    )
)
```

The error is dense, but by reading through it, you can understand that the decoding was looking for a String for the "category" key but got a dictionary instead. That's exactly the error we'd expect from the change we made in the JSON input.

One possible implementation that makes this test pass is introducing a nested private object to decode the category and forward its name to the category property:

```
// MenuItem.swift
struct MenuItem {
    let name: String
    let spicy: Bool
```

```swift
    private let categoryObject: Category

    var category: String { categoryObject.name }

    enum CodingKeys: String, CodingKey {
        case name, spicy
        case categoryObject = "category"
    }

    struct Category: Equatable, Decodable {
        let name: String
    }
}

// ...

extension MenuItem: Decodable {}

// This is required to make the existing code with the
// hardcoded menu compile.
extension MenuItem {

    init(category: String, name: String, spicy: Bool) {
        self.categoryObject = Category(name: category)
        self.name = name
        self.spicy = spicy
    }
}
```

In the case of a nontrivial JSON structure like the one in this example, I feel a test is a useful feedback mechanism to guide the decoding implementation.

Something else to keep in mind is that we always call JSON decoding as part of a network request or some other kind of data transferring; it's not something we might call directly in a ViewModel. Because the return type of the `fetchMenu` in `MenuFetching` is `AnyPublisher<[MenuItem], Error>`, a component fetching the menu from the remote API will also have to decode the received data into a `[MenuItem]`. As long as the decoding has no custom logic, the tests for the networking component will fail if something goes wrong. That is, testing the networking code implicitly exercises the JSON decoding logic.

If your API is such that you can decode it with little to no custom code, you're better off jumping straight to implementing the networking code and saving yourself the time to write tests for the decoding logic. That's because the Swift standard library takes care of the decoding; it's not your responsibility to test that.

If there is a certain amount of ad hoc decoding logic, though, like in the previous example, then a set of focused tests will help you implement it and make sure it doesn't break.

A TDD purist would be pulling their hair out and scream at me in frustration right now. How dare I suggest that it's okay not to write tests in a book about Test-Driven Development?!

Test-Driven Development is a practice, not a way of life. If the return on investment of writing some code test-first is not worth it, both in the short and long term, then it's okay not to write a test for that code.

We've wrestled with when deploying TDD is appropriate for writing JSON decoding logic and seen a couple of options on how to do so. It's now time to put this logic in action by building the final component in our feature: the one responsible for fetching the menu data from the API.

Practice Time

The API responses we've seen in the chapter have all been flat JSON arrays, meaning we can decode an array of `MenuItems` as long as `MenuItem` itself is `Decodable`. How would you decode `MenuItem` if the response was an object? For example:

```
{
    "items": [
        {
            "name": "spaghetti carbonara",
            "category": "pasta",
            "spicy": false
        },
        {
            "name": "penne all'arrabbiata",
            "category": "pasta",
            "spicy": true
        }
    ]
}
```

Key Takeaways

- **One approach to test JSON decoding logic is to define an inline String, convert it to Data, and use it as the input for JSONDecoder.** This approach is useful for input JSONs that have few keys and to make the input value to model property relationship clear.

- **Another option is to define the input in a dedicated JSON file and convert that to Data in the test.** This approach is useful for input objects with many keys but adds a layer of indirection between the input and the resulting SUT properties.

- **Keep your tests tidy by extracting the logic to convert from JSON to Data into helper functions.**

- **Testing JSON decoding logic is valuable if there is custom logic required to conform to `Decodable`**. If all the model properties match the input JSON's keys, Swift takes care of everything for us, and a test for it is redundant.

Endnote

1. There are options other than REST for an API backend. Two that are gaining more and more popularity are GraphQL and ProtoBufs. Both of them add a type-safety layer to the API, which you can – and should – leverage to code-generate all the conversion logic between API responses and application domain objects.

    ProtoBufs serializes data in a custom format that is more efficient than JSON. GraphQL responds with JSON objects, but stands out for its *query language*. Rather than having different endpoints for different resources, you ask a GraphQL backend for data by sending it a query that describes the information you need.

    In a small application like ours, the overhead of adopting either of those solutions dwarfs the benefits we would get in terms of maintainability and efficiency.

CHAPTER 10

Testing Network Code

How do you write tests for code interfacing with the network?

By sidestepping it with a Stub, to simulate different behaviors and avoid flaky tests.

A common problem faced when trying to test networking code is that the network is unpredictable and slow, resulting in non-deterministic tests — they may pass one time and fail the next.

In this chapter, we'll see how to use the *Dependency Inversion Principle* and *Stub Test Double* techniques to decouple our code from the network's real-world constraints.

The remote menu loading feature is almost complete. We built a view capable of updating when data comes in from the remote API and made the domain model `Decodable`. It's now time to implement the logic loading the data from the network. Let's call the object responsible for this `MenuFetcher`.

Apple provides an advanced and versatile system for making network calls via `URLSession` in the Foundation framework, and we shall use it for our networking implementation. We also know that `MenuFetcher` has to conform to `MenuFetching`, the abstraction we defined in Chapter 7. The `protocol` is the contract between ViewModel and lower-level components on how to fetch the menu from a remote resource.

`MenuFetching` defines the behavior we need to implement. When the request succeeds, it should return the received `Data` converted into a `[MenuItem]`. When the request fails, it should send through the error it received. Let's write the test list for `MenuFetcher` based on that spec:

```
// MenuFetcherTests.swift
@testable import Albertos
import XCTest

class MenuFetcherTests: XCTestCase {

    func testWhenRequestSucceedsPublishesDecodedMenuItems() {}

    func testWhenRequestFailsPublishesReceivedError() {}
}
```

A natural starting point here would be to hit the remote API using `URLSession` and assert the result matches our expectation.

Directly hitting the network in the unit tests is undesirable. It results in slow and flaky tests and makes it hard to exercise all of the different scenarios. Let see why and what to do about it.

Why You Shouldn't Make Network Requests in Your Unit Tests

To understand the limitations of testing direct networking, let's write such a test ourselves.

So far in the book, we've used Wishful Coding for most of our new code. Wishful Coding is useful to get started writing code when you're not sure what shape it should take, but we've worked with enough Combine by now to have a clear idea of the structure we should use. Let's begin with an incomplete implementation of `MenuFetcher` so that we can write a full test without compiler errors:

```
// MenuFetcher.swift
import Combine

class MenuFetcher: MenuFetching {
```

```swift
func fetchMenu() -> AnyPublisher<[MenuItem], Error> {
    return Future { $0(.success([]))
    }.eraseToAnyPublisher()
}
}
```

The fetching request returns an AnyPublisher<[MenuItem], Error>, which sends asynchronous updates. We already saw in Chapter 7 that we can test this kind of code by subscribing to it with sink and using an XCTestExpectation to wait for a new value:

```swift
// MenuFetcherTests.swift
// ...
func testWhenRequestSucceedsPublishesDecodeMenuItems() {
    let menuFetcher = MenuFetcher()

    let expectation = XCTestExpectation(description: "Publishes
        decoded [MenuItem]")

    menuFetcher.fetchMenu()
        .sink(
            receiveCompletion: { _ in },
            receiveValue: { items in
                // How to test if the value of items is
                // correct?
                expectation.fulfill()
            }
        )
        .store(in: &cancellables)

    wait(for: [expectation], timeout: 1)
}
```

Writing this test brings up a question: how can we assert that
MenuFetcher publishes the correct value?

Because the data comes from the remote API, the only way to know what
values to expect is to look there. Once we know what values the backend
holds, we can use some broad-stroke assertions, for example, checking that
the count is the same and that the first and last elements match.

You can find a fake version of the API at `https://github.com/`
`mokagio/tddinswift_fake_api/`. In theme with moving in small steps and
only write as little code as necessary, this fake API is actually merely a
container for JSON files. The endpoint for the menu list is nothing more
than the URL of the fake response static JSON.

Fetching static JSONs from a remote resource is an excellent way to
simulate the real-world behavior of interfacing with a fully fledged API
backend:

```
// MenuFetcherTests.swift
// ...
menuFetcher.fetchMenu()
    .sink(
        receiveCompletion: { _ in },
        receiveValue: { items in
            XCTAssertEqual(items.count, 42)
            XCTAssertEqual(items.first?.name, "spaghetti
            carbonara")
            XCTAssertEqual(items.last?.name, "pasta all'arrabbiata")
            expectation.fulfill()
        }
    )
```

It's okay to use a looser set of assertions in this instance because we
already wrote a comprehensive test for the decoding in the previous
chapter. If that wasn't the case, and the JSON decoding logic was

nontrivial, I'd encourage you to at least check that one element in the array has all the expected properties from its JSON counterpart.

Running the tests with the Cmd U keyboard shortcut will show a failure. No surprise there: our initial implementation returns a hardcoded empty array.

Let's implement a real call to the network using URLSession and Combine:

```swift
// MenuFetcher.swift
import Combine
import Foundation
class MenuFetcher: MenuFetching {

    func fetchMenu() -> AnyPublisher<[MenuItem], Error> {
        let url = URL(string:
"https://raw.githubusercontent.com/mokagio/tddinswift_fake_api/
trunk/menu_response.json")!

        URLSession.shared
            .dataTaskPublisher(for: URLRequest(url: url))
            .map { $0.data }
            .decode(type: [MenuItem].self, decoder: JSONDecoder())
            .eraseToAnyPublisher()
    }
}
```

The test should now pass. I say *should* because there are a few factors that might make it fail.

First of all, if the menu in the backend changes, the test will fail. For example, if Alberto adds a new dish, the expectation on the count will fail. **Depending on live values makes your unit tests non-deterministic and will require constant updates to the suite**. The whole point of having a dedicated API for the menu is to make updating it easier; we can expect it

155

to change many times in the future. Every time the remote menu changes, the test could fail. You might be working on a new feature and be surprised by this test failing out of the blue.

Another factor that makes this test non-deterministic is the dependency on the network. The API might respond slowly because of a poor connection or not reply at all if there is no Internet available. If that happens, the test will fail, but the cause is outside your source code.

Depending on your connection's quality, the 1 second used in `wait(for:, timeout:)` might not be enough, and the test will time out. You might need to use a longer time interval to make the test robust against slow networks, but this comes at the cost of having a slow test suite.

Even with a longer timeout, you are still susceptible to other network failures. To verify this, delete the app from your Simulator to remove any cached value, disconnect your Mac from the Internet by turning the Wi-Fi off or unplugging the Ethernet cable, and rerun the tests. The test will fail with

> Asynchronous wait failed: Exceeded timeout of 1 seconds, with unfulfilled expectations: "Publishes decoded [MenuItem]."

Interfacing with the network slows down your unit tests with the overhead of its response time. One of the advantages of Test-Driven Development is its fast feedback cycle but performing real network requests from your tests slows it down, making the whole process less effective.

Even if you're willing to go past these limitations, how can you test the code's behavior when the API request fails?

The way forward is to apply the *Dependency Inversion Principle*.

156

FORCE-UNWRAPPING OPTIONALS

You might have noticed the code obtains the URL by calling URL(string:) with a hardcoded value. URL(string:) returns an Optional value, and we use the ! suffix to force-unwrap it.

Force-unwrapping an Optional is a way to tell the Swift compiler that we trust its value will never be none at runtime and bypass the need to manually unwrap it using if let or guard let.

It's usually best to avoid force-unwrapping: if by any chance the value turns out to be none at runtime, the app will crash. It's better to write a few extra lines of code to explicitly unwrap Optionals and handle the case when they don't have a value.

While it's wise to avoid force-unwrapping, this URL(string:) call would return none only if the developer who wrote the hardcoded value made a mistake. As Chris Eidhof, Daniel Eggert, and Florian Kugler argue, this use of force-unwrapping is a useful way to expose programmer errors by making the application crash early. Since we practice TDD and most of our code is covered by tests, the chance of a crash caused by a programmer error like this one going unnoticed is slim, so we can confidently use force-unwrap in these particular cases.

How to Decouple the Unit Tests from the Network

MenuFetcher depends on URLSession to access the network. As we've seen in Chapter 7, high-level components should not depend on low-level ones; they should both depend on abstractions. That's the *Dependency Inversion Principle*.

The network is just another dependency of our system. We can place an abstraction layer between MenuFetcher and URLSession and build a *Stub Test Double* to simulate the indirect input the network provides to the SUT.

We used the URLSession dataTaskPublisher(for:) method to perform the network request, which returns an AnyPublisher<(Data, URLResponse), URLError>. The abstraction we'll define should have a similar signature, with the difference that our business logic doesn't need to read the URLResponse:

```
// NetworkFetching.swift
import Combine
import Foundation

protocol NetworkFetching {

    func load(_ request: URLRequest) -> AnyPublisher<Data,
    URLError>
}
```

We can make URLSession conform to the NetworkFetching in a thin extension:

```
// URLSession+NetworkFetching.swift
import Combine
import Foundation

extension URLSession: NetworkFetching {

    func load(_ request: URLRequest) -> AnyPublisher<Data,
    URLError> {
        return dataTaskPublisher(for: request)
            .map { $0.data }
            .eraseToAnyPublisher()
    }
}
```

It's crucial to keep the code conforming to the protocol as simple as possible and free from custom logic because we won't be testing it. With an implementation like that, all the code is outside our control because it's

Apple code. It's not our responsibility to test URLSession, and we can be relatively confident it will always behave as expected.[1]

Let's apply DIP and refactor MenuFetcher to depend on the NetworkFetching instead of calling URLSession directly:

```
// MenuFetcher.swift
import Combine
import Foundation

class MenuFetcher: MenuFetching {

    let networkFetching: NetworkFetching

    init(networkFetching: NetworkFetching = URLSession.shared) {
        self.networkFetching = networkFetching
    }

    func fetchMenu() -> AnyPublisher<[MenuItem], Error> {
        let url = URL(string:
"https://raw.githubusercontent.com/mokagio/tddinswift_fake_api/
trunk/menu_response.json")!

        networkFetching
            .load(URLRequest(url: url))
            .decode(type: [MenuItem].self, decoder:
            JSONDecoder())
            .eraseToAnyPublisher()
    }
}
```

The tests are still passing, with the caveat and limitations discussed earlier. It's now time to build a *Stub* for NetworkFetching and use it to simulate the different behaviors we want to test.

Simulate Network Requests Using a Stub

To write the tests, we need a way to provide them with a predefined input to check against: either Data to decode or a URLError value. We can build a Stub Test Double for this, using the same technique we learned in Chapter 8:

```swift
// NetworkFetchingStub.swift
@testable import Albertos
import Combine
import Foundation

class NetworkFetchingStub: NetworkFetching {

    private let result: Result<Data, URLError>

    init(returning result: Result<Data, URLError>) {
        self.result = result
    }

    func load(_ request: URLRequest) -> AnyPublisher<Data,
    URLError> {
        return result.publisher
            // Use a delay to simulate the real world async
            // behavior
            .delay(for: 0.01, scheduler: RunLoop.main)
            .eraseToAnyPublisher()
    }
}
```

We can use the Stub to decouple from the network's non-deterministic nature and have better control over the test's input:

```swift
// MenuFetcherTests.swift
// ...
func testWhenRequestSucceedsPublishesDecodedMenuItems() throws {
    let json = """
[
    { "name": "a name", "category": "a category", "spicy": true },
    { "name": "another name", "category": "a category",
    "spicy": true }
]
"""
    let data = try XCTUnwrap(json.data(using: .utf8))
    let menuFetcher = MenuFetcher(networkFetching: Network
FetchingStub(returning: .success(data)))

    let expectation = XCTestExpectation(description: "Publishes
decoded [MenuItem]")

    menuFetcher.fetchMenu()
        .sink(
            receiveCompletion: { _ in },
            receiveValue: { items in
                XCTAssertEqual(items.count, 2)
                XCTAssertEqual(items.first?.name, "a name")
                XCTAssertEqual(items.last?.name, "another
                name")
                expectation.fulfill()
            }
        )
        .store(in: &cancellables)

    wait(for: [expectation], timeout: 1)
}
```

Using the Stub removes the dependency on the network making them faster and more robust. If you try running the tests offline now, you'll see they pass.

A Stub in a networking test also helps to clarify where the values used in the assertions come from: their definition is now part of the test itself.

Let's move on to the test for failure management:

```swift
// MenuFetcherTests.swift
// ...
func testWhenRequestFailsPublishesReceivedError() {
    let expectedError = URLError(.badServerResponse)
    let menuFetcher = MenuFetcher(networkFetching: NetworkFetching
    Stub(returning: .failure(expectedError)))

    let expectation = XCTestExpectation(description: "Publishes
    received URLError")

    menuFetcher.fetchMenu()
        .sink(
            receiveCompletion: { completion in
                guard case .failure(let error) = completion else
                { return }
                XCTAssertEqual(error as? URLError, expectedError)
                expectation.fulfill()
            },
            receiveValue: { items in
                XCTFail("Expected to fail, succeeded with \(items)")
            }
        )
        .store(in: &cancellables)

    wait(for: [expectation], timeout: 1)
}
```

This test passes already. The reason for it is that we're testing the default behavior of what Combine's extension of URLSession already gives us.

Even though one could argue that this test is redundant, I'd encourage you to keep it. Ensuring that our code handles failures properly is key to building robust software with a great user experience. Having an explicit test for that signals that we take error handling seriously. The fact error handling is all done for us by Combine under the hood is an implementation detail, and it might change in the future. A dedicated test ensures that if error handling changes, you'll know about it immediately.

A Third-Party Alternative

This book only treats vanilla XCTest, but there is a third-party library worth mentioning when it comes to testing networking code: OHHTTPStubs. This library allows you to stub network requests directly on top of URLSession without the need for a dedicated abstraction layer, making it an excellent choice to add tests to big legacy codebases that are hard to change before starting to refactor them.

You can test networking logic by insulating from the network itself and focusing only on how your app makes requests and handles their result.

By defining an abstraction to hide the inner workings of URLSession, you can simulate any response from the network and write comprehensive tests using a Stub Test Double while also removing the intrinsic non-deterministic effect making real HTTP requests introduces.

Keep the code conforming to the abstraction layer to a minimum, ideally using only methods provided by Apple. You can be confident in its correct behavior, even though you didn't write a test for it.

Practice Time

Imagine the API had another endpoint for the "dish of the day," which returns a single item. How would you implement reading from that endpoint using Test-Driven Development? Would you add the functionality to MenuFetching or create a new dedicated abstraction? Would NetworkFetchingStub need changes, or would it be ready to support this test too?

You can find the response for this endpoint at https://raw. githubusercontent.com/mokagio/tddinswift_fake_api/trunk/dish_ of_the_day.json.

Here's another exercise for you. Currently, MenuFetcher uses a hardcoded value as the API endpoint. Hardcoded values are useful to get started quickly, but they're not flexible. You cannot, for example, have one version of the app contacting the staging and one the production backend with a hardcoded URL.

A better approach would be to initialize MenuFetcher with a base URL parameter to make it agnostic of where the API is deployed. Internally, MenuFetcher can construct the endpoint URL by appending the appropriate path to the base value. What tests can you write to implement this refinement?

Hint   Modify the Stub to expect a URLRequest and Result pair and only return the given Result when the URLRequest passed to load(_:) matches the given one.

Key Takeaways

- **Do not make network requests in your unit tests**. Hitting the network makes your tests non-deterministic and slower because of its real-world physical constraints.

- **Define an abstraction layer to decouple your source and test code from the lower-level networking implementation**. By applying the Dependency Inversion Principle, you'll shape a more modular software and be able to use Test Doubles.

- **Use as thin a wrapper as possible around `URLSession`**. Because you cannot directly test that code, it should be as minimal and simple as possible.

- **Use a Stub Test Double to simulate successful and failure responses coming from the network**. With a Stub, you can provide any kind of input to your networking component.

Endnote

1. If you wanted to go the extra mile and have a
   security check on the URLSession behavior, you
   could write an *integration* test exercising the
   NetworkFetching method implementation on
   URLSession. As we've seen, interfacing with the
   real network makes the test non-deterministic and
   slower. This test should live in a dedicated target
   that doesn't run together with the unit tests. You
   can use it whenever you upgrade to a new version of
   Xcode as a safety check.

CHAPTER 11

Injecting Dependencies with @EnvironmentObject

How do you share the same instance of an object between SwiftUI views without injecting it through all their common ancestors in the view hierarchy?

By using @EnvironmentObject to access it from the environment, the context in which all the views live.

In this chapter, you'll learn how to share business logic components between views with @EnvironmentObject in a testable way.

Our app is getting closer to being fully functional. To get there, we need to build the UI and business logic to let customers select dishes and make their orders.

What's the Earliest Testable ordering functionality we can build? We can start with merely adding and removing items to and from the order and show users their order on a screen with a read-only view, as illustrated in Figure 11-1. From that screen, they'll eventually be able to submit a payment. Let's work on the order building and showing in this chapter, leaving the submission for the next.

© Gio Lodi 2021
G. Lodi, *Test-Driven Development in Swift*, https://doi.org/10.1007/978-1-4842-7002-8_11

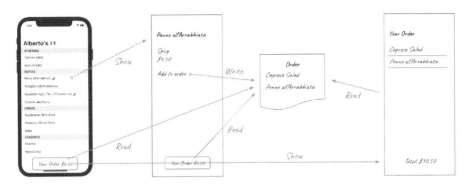

Figure 11-1. *The ordering flow*

For customers to assemble their order by selecting dishes from the menu, we'll need:

- A detail screen for each menu item, including its price, and a button to add it to the order

- A screen showing the order summary and a button to submit it

- An object to hold and update the order model

Let's start from the object in charge of providing an interface and coordinating updates to the order, which we shall call OrderController.

The implementation details of OrderController are not interesting for this chapter, only its interface. I'll leave building it with TDD as an exercise for you. You can find a version in the source code that comes with this book.

Here are the interfaces for OrderController and its Order model:

```
// Order.swift
struct Order {

    let items: [MenuItem]

    var total: Double { ... }
}
```

```
// OrderController.swift
import Combine

class OrderController: ObservableObject {

    @Published private(set) var order: Order

    init(order: Order = Order(items: [])) { ... }

    func isItemInOrder(_ item: MenuItem) -> Bool { ... }

    func addToOrder(item: MenuItem) { ... }

    func removeFromOrder(item: MenuItem) { ... }
}
```

You'll find the initial version of MenuItemDetail, OrderButton, and OrderDetail views and their ViewModels in this chapter's companion source code.

To access the same order, the views need to interact with the same instance of OrderController. MenuItemDetail.ViewModel will use OrderController to add or remove its item to or from the order, OrderButton.ViewModel to show the total amount, and OrderDetail. ViewModel to read and show the items in the order. We need a way to share the same reference between all these components.

One option could be defining a static instance in the global namespace or as a sharedInstance property on the OrderController type itself. It would solve the problem of sharing the same value across multiple objects, but how could we write tests for it?

The behavior depends on the state of the Order held by OrderController: if all the tests modify the same shared instance, the way a test leaves the order will affect the next test's result. The tests lose their isolation and become dependent on each other. When the operation a test performs changes the result of another test, the suite becomes brittle and hard to work with.

To test each ViewModel in isolation, we need to use a different `OrderController` instance in each.

As we've already discussed, *Dependency Injection* is the technique of providing an object or a method with all its dependencies without requiring it to create them in its implementation.

By injecting the `OrderController` dependency into each ViewModel, we'll be able to test them in isolation. We can then use the @`EnvironmentObject` property wrapper that SwiftUI provides to access a shared instance of `OrderController` when instantiating the ViewModels.

Let's see how this works in practice by working on adding and removing the order to and from the new menu item screen.

How Dependency Injection Keeps Each Test Isolated

Here's the test list for how `MenuItemDetail.ViewModel` should manage the button to update the order through `OrderController`:

```
// MenuItemDetail.ViewModelTests.swift
// ...
func testWhenItemIsInOrderButtonSaysRemove() {}

func testWhenItemIsNotInOrderButtonSaysAdd() {}

func testWhenItemIsInOrderButtonActionRemovesIt() {}

func testWhenItemIsNotInOrderButtonActionAddsIt() {}
```

Let's start with the test for the button text value when the ViewModel's item is already in the order:

```
func testWhenItemIsInOrderButtonSaysRemove() {
    // Arrange inputs
    // Act by reading the button text from the ViewModel

    XCTAssertEqual(text, "Remove from order")
}
```

Where does the text we are checking come from? From a property of the ViewModel, the one the View will eventually read:

```
func testWhenItemIsInOrderButtonSaysRemove() {
    // Arrange inputs

    let text = viewModel.addOrRemoveFromOrderButtonText()

    XCTAssertEqual(text, "Remove from order")
}
```

MenuItemDetail.ViewModel needs a MenuItem to show and the OrderController to use to check if the item is in the order. The state that should result in the "Remove from order" text requires that the input MenuItem is part of the order stored in OrderController:

```
func testWhenItemIsInOrderButtonSaysRemove() {
    let item = MenuItem.fixture()
    let orderController = OrderController()
    orderController.addToOrder(item: item)
    let viewModel = MenuItemDetail.ViewModel(item: item,
    orderController: orderController)
        // Compiler says: Extra argument 'orderController' in call

    let text = viewModel.addOrRemoveFromOrderButtonText

    XCTAssertEqual(text, "Remove from order")
}
```

Let's update the ViewModel with the simplest code that can make the test compile and pass:

```swift
// MenuItemDetail.ViewModel.swift
// ...
extension MenuItemDetail {

    struct ViewModel {
        // ...
        let addOrRemoveFromOrderButtonText = "Remove from order"

        private let orderController: OrderController

        // TODO: Using default value for OrderController while
        // working on the ViewModel implementation.
        // We'll remove it once done and inject it from the view.
        init(item: MenuItem, orderController: OrderController =
        OrderController()) {
            self.item = item
            self.orderController = orderController
            // ...
        }
    }
}
```

Notice how I used a default value for the `OrderController` parameter. A default value saves us from updating the view to pass the correct value to its ViewModel: extra work that would only delay the feedback cycle. It's better to stay focused on the ViewModel, make it work properly, and only then move on updating the view.

I also added a comment prefixed with `"TODO"` to note the compromise made by using the default value.

`TODO` comments are a way to leave reminders in the codebase. You can use a script or a tool like SwiftLint to add a Build Phase Run Script step that generates warnings for each `TODO` comment, so you won't forget about them.

TODOs are great to leave yourself quick notes while in the TDD flow, but you should address all of them before considering your work finished. Avoid opening pull requests against your main branch that have TODOs in them. If you can't take care of a TODO because it's out of scope or you are waiting on something else, then move it to your project management system: leftover TODO warnings create extra noise in the codebase that could hide new genuine warnings.

If you now run the tests for MenuItemDetail.ViewModel using the Ctrl Option Cmd U keyboard shortcut, you'll see they pass.

With a green baseline established, we can now refactor the ViewModel implementation to be an ObservableObject that publishes its addOrRemoveFromOrderButtonText property, so the view will automatically update as the user adds or removes the item to or from their order:

```
// MenuItemDetail.ViewModel.swift
import Combine

extension MenuItemDetail {

    class ViewModel: ObservableObject {
        // ...
        @Published private(set) var addOrRemoveFromOrderButtonText
        = "Remove from order"
        // ...
}
```

If we rerun the tests using the Ctrl Option Cmd G keyboard shortcut, we can see they still pass. There isn't any real logic, though: the property value is hardcoded. Writing the test for when the item is not in the order will force us to come up with a real implementation:

```
// MenuItemDetail.ViewModelTests.swift
// ...
func testWhenItemIsNotInOrderButtonSaysAdd() {
    let item = MenuItem.fixture()
```

```
    let orderController = OrderController()
    let viewModel = MenuItemDetail.ViewModel(item: item,
    orderController: orderController)

    let text = viewModel.addOrRemoveFromOrderButtonText

    XCTAssertEqual(text, "Add to order")
}
```

Here's how to make the test pass:

```
// MenuItemDetail.ViewModel.swift
// ...
extension MenuItemDetail {

    class ViewModel: ObservableObject {
        // ...
        private var cancellables = Set<AnyCancellable>()

        // TODO: Using default value for OrderController while
        // Working on the ViewModel implementation.
        // We'll remove it once done and inject it from the view.
        init(item: MenuItem, orderController: OrderController =
        OrderController()) {
            // ...
            self.orderController.$order
                .sink { [weak self] order in
                    guard let self = self else { return }

                    if (order.items.contains { $0 == self.item
                    }) {
                        self.addOrRemoveFromOrderButtonText =
                        "Remove from order"
```

```
        } else {
            self.addOrRemoveFromOrderButtonText =
            "Add to order"
        }
    }
    .store(in: &cancellables)
}
}
}
```

The approach is the same for the method holding the action for `Button` to perform in the view layer:

```
// MenuItemDetail.ViewModelTests.swift
func testWhenItemIsInOrderButtonActionRemovesIt() {
    let item = MenuItem.fixture()
    let orderController = OrderController()
    orderController.addToOrder(item: item)
    let viewModel = MenuItemDetail.ViewModel(item: item,
    orderController: orderController)

    viewModel.addOrRemoveFromOrder()

    XCTAssertFalse(orderController.order.items.contains { $0 ==
    item })
}

func testWhenItemIsNotInOrderButtonActionAddsIt() {
    let item = MenuItem.fixture()
    let orderController = OrderController()
    let viewModel = MenuItemDetail.ViewModel(item: item,
    orderController: orderController)

    viewModel.addOrRemoveFromOrder()
```

```
    XCTAssertTrue(orderController.order.items.contains {
    $0 == item })
}

// MenuItemDetail.ViewModel.swift
func addOrRemoveFromOrder() {
    if (orderController.order.items.contains { $0 == item }) {
        orderController.removeFromOrder(item: item)
    } else {
        orderController.addToOrder(item: item)
    }
}
```

Dependency Injection vs. Directly Accessing Shared Instances

How is using Dependency Injection better than having a shared OrderController and accessing it within the ViewModel implementation? Because with the latter each test would update the same Order, coupling the result of a test to work done by those before it.

To verify that, you can define a shared OrderController instance like this:

```
// OrderController.swift
// ...
class OrderController: ObservableObject {

    static let shared = OrderController()
    // ...
}
```

Update MenuItemDetail.ViewModel to access the shared instance instead of the parameter from its init by replacing any self. orderController occurrence access with OrderController.shared.

Next, update the assertions for the button action behavior to check the value from the shared instance. Now run the tests and notice how they fail.

You can work around those failures by adding `setUp` and `tearDown` calls that restore `OrderController.shared` to a clean state before each test. Another option is to order the tests so that the way one updates `OrderController` leaves it in the state the next one expects. Both alternatives require extra work and make the test setup more rigid; using Dependency Injection is a much better option.

Dependency Injection makes your code honest. Shared instances and singletons allow your objects to get hold of and interact with components that their interfaces do not declare. As Miško Hevery puts it, they make your API into a *pathological liar*. In a codebase where freely reading from the global state is allowed, you cannot trust that the methods you call have no side effects or collaborate only with the dependencies in their signatures unless you inspect their implementation. Reasoning about code becomes challenging because you're never sure if methods do what they say they do or if there's more going on under the hood.

TDD nudges you toward using Dependency Injection. Writing your code starting by its tests is easier if you pass all the dependencies instead of accessing them in the implementation. The software design that emerges from the necessity of writing tests first and getting feedback fast has only explicit dependencies and is, therefore, more straightforward to reason about.

The ViewModel implementation is now complete. It's time to wire it up with the view layer.

Dependency Injection with `@EnvironmentObject`

`MenuItemDetail.ViewModel` works in isolation, but, as the `TODO` comment reminds us, it's using a dedicated `OrderController` instance, not a shared one. We need to instantiate `MenuItemDetail.ViewModel` with a reference to the same `OrderController` that the rest of the application will use.

MenuList is responsible for creating a MenuItemDetail and its ViewModel when the user selects an item, so it's up to it to pass an OrderController instance. How can MenuList get a hold of one? We could apply the same reasoning and make the component responsible for creating MenuList give it the OrderController instance it needs for MenuItemDetail. AlbertosApp creates MenuList, and since it's the top-level element in the view hierarchy, we can make it build and hold the OrderController value to share through the app.

As we've already discussed, this approach is not ideal. It might seem alright in the relatively flat view hierarchy of Alberto's app, but you can see how it's a slippery slope: the deeper and richer your view hierarchy, the more code you'll have to write to pass dependencies down through it. On top of that, making MenuList require an OrderController in its init can give the false impression that it needs to use it, while it's merely passing it along without ever interacting with it.

SwiftUI's @EnvironmentObject helps growing applications without bloating the view hierarchy with long Dependency Injection chains. Views can use this property wrapper to load an ObservableObject-conforming property value from their environment. We can register objects in the environment with the environmetObject(_:) method in one ancestor of the view accessing it.

@EnvironmentObject lets us cleanly share access to shared objects without having to pass them through each view hierarchy layer. The ViewModels that need to read from or interact with OrderController can request a reference as part of their init parameters. The views that instantiate them can provide the shared instance by fetching it from the environment via @EnvironmentObject.

Let's start by updating MenuItemDetail to use the new logic from its ViewModel to drive the button's behavior:

```swift
// MenuItemDetail.swift
import SwiftUI

struct MenuItemDetail: View {

    @ObservedObject private(set) var viewModel: ViewModel

    var body: some View {
        // ...
        Button(viewModel.addOrRemoveFromOrderButtonText) {
            viewModel.addOrRemoveFromOrder()
        }
        // ...
    }
}
```

If you run the app now, you'll see that the "Add to order" button changes to "Remove from order" when clicked. Once again, we got to a working app on our first attempt, thanks to TDD.

Let's move on to addressing the TODO comment we left earlier and remove the default OrderController value:

```swift
// MenuItemDetail.ViewModel.swift
init(item: MenuItem, orderController: OrderController) {
    // ...
}
```

The compiler now cannot build MenuList:

```swift
// MenuList.swift
var body: some View {
    // ...
    List {
        ForEach(sections) { section in
            Section(header: Text(section.category)) {
                ForEach(section.items) { item in
```

```
                    NavigationLink(destination:
                    MenuItemDetail(viewModel: .init(item: item))) {
                        // Compiler says: Missing argument for
                        // parameter 'orderController' in call
```

Let's get a reference to `OrderController` from the environment and instantiate the ViewModel with it:

```
// MenuList.swift
// ...
@EnvironmentObject var orderController: OrderController

var body: some View {
    // ...
    List {
        ForEach(sections) { section in
            Section(header: Text(section.category)) {
                ForEach(section.items) { item in
                    NavigationLink(destination:
                    destination(for: item)) {
                        // ...

func destination(for item: MenuItem) -> MenuItemDetail {
    return MenuItemDetail(viewModel: .init(item: item,
    orderController: orderController))
}
```

The app now compiles, but if you run it, you'll see that it crashes:

Fatal error: No `ObservableObject` of type `OrderController` found. A `View.environmentObject(_:)` for `OrderController` may be missing as an ancestor of this view

The Downside of `@EnvironmentObject`

The crash message we just received is clear on what went wrong: we didn't call `environmentObject(_:)` on an ancestor of `MenuList`. When the SwiftUI runtime tried to access the `OrderController` property, it didn't find it and crashed.

The chance of crashing is a downside of using `@EnvironmentObject`. If you forget to call `environmentObject(_:)` or if someone accidentally removes an existing call, the app will crash.

In practice, though, it's unlikely you'll ship code that doesn't register a value for each `@EnvironmentObject`. The kind of crash that comes with it is something you would immediately notice when doing a manual pass of your finished feature.

You *could* use a different approach to creating ViewModels that passes their dependencies without using `@EnvironmentObject`. For example, you could use a ViewModel factory object that instantiates and holds all of the dependencies and that the views can use to get a prebuilt ViewModel. This option, though, requires extra work and "fights" against the framework.

`@EnvironmentObject` is an API too convenient not to use it.

Besides, this kind of crash can only occur as the result of a developer error. As we've elaborated in Chapter 10 in the context of force-unwrapping the return value of a `URL(string:)` call when the string is hardcoded, an early crash in development is an acceptable way to notice a developer error.

You are better off investing in automation and processes to catch missing `environmentObject(_:)` calls rather than using a different Dependency Injection strategy.

The final step to make the app work properly is to register an
OrderController in the view environment. The best place to do this is in
the root view component:

```swift
// AlbertosApp.swift
import SwiftUI @main

struct AlbertosApp: App {
    let orderController = OrderController()

    var body: some Scene {
        WindowGroup {
            NavigationView {
                MenuList(
                    viewModel: .init(
                        menuFetching: MenuFetcher()
                    )
                )
                .navigationTitle("Alberto's ▨")
            }
            .environmentObject(orderController)
        }
    }
}
```

@EnvironmentObject vs. Directly Accessing Shared Instances

Using @EnvironmentObject looks deceivingly similar to accessing a shared
instance in the view's implementation detail.

The difference is that @EnvironmentObject is constrained to work
with SwiftUI views; if you try to access a value via this property wrapper
on a type that is not a view, the app will crash. In our Test-Driven

Development approach to SwiftUI, views are thin components free from any presentation logic. While it's true that using `@EnvironmentObject` lets them access values under the hood, they only use them to initialize their subviews' ViewModels.

On top of that, remember that we need to explicitly register objects in the environment with `environmentObject(_:)`. If you register all of the shared objects in your `App` implementation, there will always be a single place where to go and discover everything available in the environment. By contrast, there is no straightforward way to learn how many shared instance properties are available and how many the app actually accesses.

As our application grows, the number of view and business logic components will grow with it. Many small self-contained view components are more comfortable to work with in isolation but also make for a deep and intricate view hierarchy. Manually passing every dependency a view needs to do its job through such hierarchy becomes cumbersome and hard to maintain.

`@EnvironmentObject` makes providing views their dependency clean and straightforward to maintain, regardless of their depth in the hierarchy.

The menu item detail screen is now complete. Figure 11-2 shows the order flow from Figure 11-1 with the new screens instead of their placeholders.

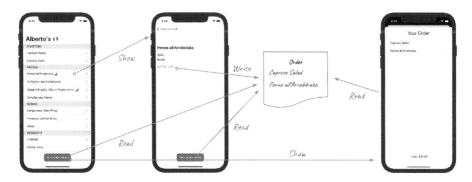

Figure 11-2. *The order flow through the app with the production screens*

The process to update the remaining views is similar, so I'll leave it as an exercise for you. In this chapter, we gave the user a way to compose their order; in the next, we'll give them a way to pay for it.

Practice Time

Once the order changes state, both `OrderButton` and `OrderDetail` should reflect it. `OrderButton`'s text should be "Your Order" when the customer hasn't selected anything and "Your Order $ `<order total>`" when there are items in the order. The list of dishes and the total price summary in `OrderDetail` should also reflect changes in the order state.

To do that, both ViewModels should expect an `OrderController` reference and use it to read that information.

Implement that using the `@EnvironmentObject` injection approach.

Key Takeaways

- **Use Dependency Injection to share the same object with different components instead of letting them access a shared instance internally**. DI makes your code easier to test and reason about by making all of its dependencies explicit.

- **Use `@EnvironmentObject` to get a reference to a shared resource in a `SwiftUI` view**. This property wrapper allows you to inject dependencies to components that are deep in the view hierarchy without passing them through all the ancestors.

- **The view instantiating a child view's ViewModel can provide it with its dependencies using `@EnvironmentObject`**.

CHAPTER 12

Testing Side Effects

How do you write tests for a system that does not return an output but changes another object's state instead?

By spying on the object affected by the SUT.

If you have control over the object on which the side effect occurs, you can inspect its state to verify it matches your expectation, but what if you don't? For example, how can you verify that an object calls a method on a third-party SDK as a result of a particular operation?

This chapter introduces a new kind of Test Double that allows us to do precisely that: the *Spy*. Using a Spy, you can replace a real dependency of your SUT with one that records which method calls it receives and the arguments passed to them, so you can assert the interaction occurred as expected.

We've come a long way since starting to work on Alberto's app. One test at a time, we went from an app showing a hardcoded menu to one that loads it from a remote API and allows customers to select the dishes they want to order.

The final piece of the puzzle is to submit the order and pay for it. Figure 12-1 shows the payment flow: when the user clicks the checkout button, the app submits the order to a remote service that processes the payment and queues it in the kitchen. When the service finishes, the app notifies the user of the result. Using an alert is a simple way to show the outcome on-screen. It's an application of the Partition Problem and Solve

Sequentially technique. First, build a working version of the flow, and then you can iterate and refine its UX.

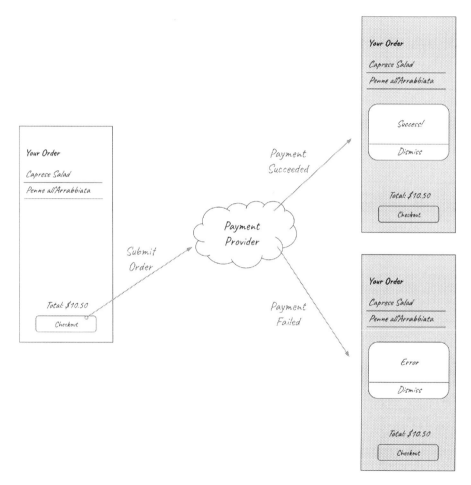

Figure 12-1. *The payment flow*

Managing payments is notoriously hard: there are required safety measures and different vendors that users expect available from the get-go. As a one-person shop, you decide to outsource the responsibility of managing payments to a third-party service.

Hippo Payments, the provider you chose, offers a Swift SDK to manage all your payments as a black box; you call it, and it takes care of authentication, vendor selection, and fulfillment.

Here's the Hippo Payments SDK interface:

```
class HippoPaymentsProcessor {

    init(apiKey: String)

    func processPayment(
        payload: [String : Any],
        onSuccess: @escaping () -> Void,
        onFailure: @escaping (HippoPaymentsError) -> Void
    )
}
```

We can add a button to the OrderDetail view that, when tapped, triggers the payment flow, eventually calling the processPayment from the SDK.

The test list for this behavior consists of a single test:

```
// OrderDetail.ViewModelTests.swift
// ...
func testWhenCheckoutButtonTappedStartsPaymentProcessingFlow() {}
```

The implementation can be similar to what we did for the user interaction: pass an SDK instance to OrderDetail.ViewModel and expose a method for OrderDetail to use as the button action with the logic to call the SDK.

How can we test that the checkout button action starts the payment flow when that doesn't result in any visible state change in HippoPaymentProcessing?

Let's update OrderDetail.ViewModel's init to expect a HippoPaymentsProcessor and see if that gives us a hint. Experimenting is a great way to get unstuck when solving a coding problem. Our comprehensive test suite grants us the freedom and confidence to play with our codebase.

Third-Party Dependencies Are the Same As All Dependencies

Here's how the ViewModel would look like with a HippoPaymentsProcessor init parameter and property:

```swift
// OrderDetail.ViewModel.swift
import Combine
import HippoPayments

extension OrderDetail {

    struct ViewModel {

        // ...
        private let paymentProcessor: HippoPaymentsProcessor
        // ...

        // TODO: Using a default value for HippoPaymentsProcessor
        // only to make the code compile.
        // We'll remove it once fully integrated.
        init(
            orderController: OrderController,
            paymentProcessor: HippoPaymentsProcessor =
            .init(apiKey: "A1B2C3")
        ) {
            self.paymentProcessor = paymentProcessor
            // ...
```

If you didn't know that HippoPaymentsProcessor comes from a different Swift module than the rest of the code, would you say there's something different between it and OrderController?

From OrderDetail.ViewModel's point of view, there is no difference between first- and third-party dependencies: they are both external objects.

CHAPTER 12   TESTING SIDE EFFECTS

Third-party dependencies are no different from first-party dependencies or Apple frameworks, and the Dependency Injection Principle applies to them, too. If third-party dependencies are no different than other dependencies, then we can apply the same playbook for testing code interacting with them: define an abstraction layer and build a Test Double.

The Benefit of Abstracting Third-Party Dependencies

Abstracting third-party dependencies is particularly beneficial because it makes it easier to migrate from one vendor to another. If you can abstract the implementation details of a particular vendor behind a `protocol` specific to your domain, adopting a different option will only be a matter of making it conform to the `protocol` too.

Another advantage is that, because you are in control of how the abstraction layer looks like, you can make third-party dependencies fit your codebase style. `HippoPaymentsProcessor` has two closure parameters for success and failure handlers, but the codebase uses Combine `Publisher`s to manage asynchronous work. We can define our abstraction layer with our favorite ergonomics and then extend `HippoPaymentsProcessor` to conform to it.

Build Wrappers for Third-Party Dependencies

```swift
// PaymentProcessing.swift
import Combine

protocol PaymentProcessing {
    func process(order: Order) -> AnyPublisher<Void, Error>
}
```

To make HippoPaymentsProcessor conform to PaymentProcessing, we can use Combine's Future type:

```
// HippoPaymentsProcessor+PaymentProcessing.swift
import Combine
import HippoPayments

extension HippoPaymentsProcessor: PaymentProcessing {

    func process(order: Order) -> AnyPublisher<Void, Error> {
        return Future { promise in
            self.processPayment(
                payload: ???,
                onSuccess: { promise(.success(())) },
                onFailure: { promise(.failure($0)) }
            )
        }
        .eraseToAnyPublisher()
    }
}
```

What should we use for the payload value? Let's pretend the SDK documentation says it should be a dictionary with an array of all the items' names in the order under the "items" key:

```
[ "items": [ "Arancini Balls", "Penne all'Arrabbiata" ] ]
```

We need a test to guide us through the payload logic implementation. We can't write a test for HippoPaymentsProcessor directly, so let's build this functionality someplace we control:

```
// Order+HippoPayments.swift
extension Order {

    var hippoPaymentsPayload: [String: Any] { [:] }
}
```

We can use TDD for this logic, which I'll leave as an exercise for you.

Now, let's update `OrderDetail.ViewModel` to expect a type conforming to `PaymentProcessing` instead of a concrete `HippoPaymentsProcessor` instance. Doing so is an application of the Dependency Inversion Principle – we are making the different components depend upon abstractions instead of concrete types:

```swift
// OrderDetail.ViewModel.swift
extension OrderDetail {

    struct ViewModel {
    // ...

    // TODO: Using a default value for HippoPaymentsProcessor
    // only to make the code compile.
    // We'll remove it once fully integrated.
    init(
        orderController: OrderController,
        paymentProcessor: PaymentProcessing =
        HippoPaymentsProcessor.init(apiKey: "A1B2C3")
    ) {
        // ...
```

Thanks to Dependency Inversion, we can now build a Test Double to verify the checkout button action starts the payment flow.

The Spy Test Double

How can we verify that clicking the checkout button starts the payment's flow in the `OrderDetail.ViewModelTests`?

We don't have access to `HippoPaymentsProcessor` to check its state or whether it sent a request to its backend. Besides, we already discussed the disadvantages of making real network requests in our tests in

Chapter 10. We don't have a way to check for changes in the application state either, since we are testing the ViewModel in isolation. What we *can* do is leverage the abstraction we put in place as a seam to insert something we can control in the tests.

We can write a Test Double conforming to `PaymentProcessing` that registers calls to the method to start the flow that we can then inspect: a *Spy*. The name Spy refers to the double "spying" on how consumers call the dependency:

```swift
// PaymentProcessingSpy.swift
@testable import Albertos
import Combine

class PaymentProcessingSpy: PaymentProcessing {

    private(set) var receivedOrder: Order?

    func process(order: Order) -> AnyPublisher<Void, Error> {
        receivedOrder = order

        return Result<Void, Error>.success(()).publisher.
        eraseToAnyPublisher()
    }
}
```

We can write a test that uses the Spy to verify the desired behavior:

```swift
// OrderDetail.ViewModelTests.swift
func testWhenCheckoutButtonTappedStartsPaymentProcessingFlow() {
    // Create an OrderController and add some items to it
    let orderController = OrderController()
    orderController.addToOrder(item: .fixture(name: "name"))
    orderController.addToOrder(item: .fixture(name: "other name"))
    // Create the Spy
    let paymentProcessingSpy = PaymentProcessingSpy()
```

```
let viewModel = OrderDetail.ViewModel(
    orderController: orderController,
    paymentProcessor: paymentProcessingSpy
)

viewModel.checkout()

XCTAssertEqual(paymentProcessingSpy.receivedOrder,
orderController.order)
}
```

To make the test pass, we only need to call the process(order:)
method from the view model:

```
// OrderDetail.ViewModel.swift

func checkout() {
    paymentProcessor.process(order: orderController.order)
}
```

The test passes, but Xcode gives us a warning: "Result of call to
'process(order:)' is unused." That's a good reminder that even though
we fired the call to process the order, we do not inform the user about its
result. We'll take care of that in the next chapter.

Next, let's update OrderDetail with a button using the new logic we
wrote:

```
// OrderDetail.swift
// ...
struct OrderDetail: View {
    // ...
    var body: some View {
        VStack(alignment: .center, spacing: 8) {
            // ...
```

```
Button {
    viewModel.checkout()
} label: {
    Text(viewModel.checkoutButtonText)
        .font(.callout)
        .bold()
        .padding(12)
        .foregroundColor(.white)
        .background(Color.crimson)
        .cornerRadius(10.0)
}
// ...
```

The Downside of Using Spies

Thanks to the Spy, we implemented and verified the order submission and payment initiation behavior.

Spies are a useful tool to verify behavior that results in method calls or internal state changes in other objects. Using a Spy has a downside, though: it tightly couples the test with the code's implementation details.

A key rule for writing maintainable tests is that you should *test behavior, not implementation.* A test focused on behavior allows you to refactor the implementation many times, but one that depends too much on implementation details will break as soon as you start refactoring. To get the most value out of your test suite, keep it focused on asserting behavior.

Spies go against the behavior-vs.-implementation guideline because they depend entirely on the interface of the type they duplicate.

That's why you should reach for a Spy, or any other Test Double for the matter, only when there is no other design option left available. In this chapter's example, there was no way to implement our behavior via a method returning a value nor a way to ask `HippoPaymentsProcessor` whether the processing started, so using a Spy was the only option left.

Practice Time

Imagine you want to log events from the app to run analytics, such as tracking the ratio between the times patrons look at an item's details and the times they order it. To do that, you decide to use Hippo Payments' sister product, Hippo Analytics, which you'll find in this chapter's companion source code.

How would you use TDD to integrate events and make sure they log the correct data?

Key Takeaways

- **You can apply the Dependency Inversion Principle to third-party dependencies like you would for first-party ones**.

- **Abstracting third-party dependencies makes it easier to change vendors and allows you to use an API in line with the rest of your codebase**. When you make a third-party SDK conform to your abstraction, you can make it adopt your codebase's coding style.

- **Use a Spy Test Double to ensure your components interact with the third-party as expected**. With a Spy, you can record method calls and state changes to verify they occur as desired.

CHAPTER 13

Testing a Conditional View Presentation

How do you test conditional logic to present a view when its code needs to live in the SwiftUI layer?

By extracting as much of it as possible in the ViewModel layer and keep the SwiftUI implementation thin.

Sometimes, presenting a view is straightforward, such as loading the detail screen when selecting an item from a list. Other times, there is logic involved, like when the user should see a different alert based on an operation's result.

Whenever there's logic involved in presenting a view, using tests to drive its implementation is the best way to make sure it's correct, and far more efficient than keeping the logic in the UI and manually verifying it.

In this chapter, we'll learn how to use Test-Driven Development to present a different `Alert` depending on the payment processing result. To do so, we'll move the core of the conditional logic at the ViewModel level and build on top of SwiftUI's `Binding` mechanism to modify the view's presentation state.

© Gio Lodi 2021
G. Lodi, *Test-Driven Development in Swift*, https://doi.org/10.1007/978-1-4842-7002-8_13

Informing the User of the Checkout Completion

In the previous chapter, we wrote the code starting the order processing flow by making `OrderDetail.ViewModel`'s `checkout()` method call `PaymentProcessing`'s `process(order:)` with the `Order` stored in the `OrderController`.

We need a way to notify the user of their order's outcome: whether the payment was successful and the kitchen received it or there was an error in the flow.

Test-Driven Development is all about small iterations. What's an Earliest Testable version of this flow? We could start by simply showing an alert after the payment completes.

SwiftUI has a dedicated type and APIs for showing alerts. The simplest way to present an alert is to have a `@State` wrapped property in the `View` representing whether it should be on-screen and then use the `View` method `alert(isPresented:, content:)` to define the `Alert` to present if the property is `true`:

```
struct ExampleView: View {

    @State var showingAlert = false

    var body: some View {
        Button {
            self.showingAlert.toggle()
        } label: {
            Text("Show Alert")
        }
        .alert(isPresented: $showingAlert) {
            Alert(
                title: Text("Hello"),
                message: Text("Hi, I'm an alert"),
```

```
                dismissButton: .default(Text("Bye"))
            )
        }
    }
}
```

alert(isPresented:, content:) expects the value of isPresented to be a Binding<Bool>. Binding<Value> is a SwiftUI type and property wrapper that creates "a two-way connection between a property that stores data and a view that displays and changes the data."

With Binding, the Alert can change the value of showingAlert once the user clicks the dismiss button.

The option we just discussed is a good introduction to presenting alerts but has all of the intelligence in the view and doesn't allow conditional logic. To present a different alert based on the result of the payment processing, we can use the more refined alert(item:, content:) API. alert(item:, content:) expects item to be a Binding<Optional <Identifiable>>. The Binding wrapper allows SwiftUI to update the wrapped value from the alert view once presented or dismissed. The Optional tells the framework that when the value changes from none to some, it should present the alert. The content parameter has to be a (Identifiable) -> Alert closure and SwiftUI will call it to get the Alert to show.

Thanks to this API, we can extract all of the conditional logic involved in presenting the alert in types detached from SwiftUI, allowing us to use Test-Driven Development to build them.

1. Define a ViewModel for the alert.

2. Add a @Published property to OrderDetail.
    ViewModel with an Optional alert ViewModel.

3. Make OrderDetail.ViewModel update this property
    based on the result of the payment processing.

4.   Make OrderDetail read the Binding value
associated with the @Published property (using the
$ prefix).

The ViewModel for the alert can be a plain struct:

```swift
// Alert.ViewModel.swift
import SwiftUI

extension Alert {

    struct ViewModel: Identifiable {
        let title: String
        let message: String
        let buttonText: String

        var id: String { title + message + buttonText }
    }
}
```

The next step is to add an Alert.ViewModel @Published property to
OrderDetail.ViewModel:

```swift
// OrderDetail.ViewModel.swift
// ...
extension OrderDetail {

    class ViewModel: ObservableObject {
        // ...

        @Published private(set) var alertToShow: Alert.
        ViewModel?

        // ...
    }
}
```

If you build the code for testing after this change using the Shift Cmd U keyboard shortcut, you'll see that it still compiles even though we didn't update the init method of OrderDetail.ViewModel. The reason is that the Swift compiler can infer the default value of an Optional variable, like var alertToShow: Alert.ViewModel?, to be none. That's precisely the value we want because we should show the alert only once the payment processing finishes.

Let's write the test list for this behavior:

```
// OrderDetail.ViewModelTests.swift
@testable import Albertos
import XCTest

class OrderDetailViewModelTests: XCTestCase {

    // ...

    func testWhenPaymentSucceedsUpdatesPropertyToShowConfirmation
    Alert() {}

    func testWhenPaymentFailsUpdatesPropertyToShowErrorAlert() {}
}
```

Let's begin with the failure scenario to ensure we give error handling the care it deserves.

To test that the payment processing fails, we need to simulate this scenario in the PaymentProcessing dependency. We can do that using a Stub Test Double, as we learned in Chapter 8:

```
// PaymentProcessingStub.swift
@testable import Albertos
import Combine
import Foundation
```

```
class PaymentProcessingStub: PaymentProcessing {

    let result: Result<Void, Error>

    init(returning result: Result<Void, Error>) {
        self.result = result
    }

    func process(order: Order) -> AnyPublisher<Void, Error> {
        return result.publisher
            // Use a delay to simulate the real world async
            // behavior
            .delay(for: 0.01, scheduler: RunLoop.main)
            .eraseToAnyPublisher()
    }
}
```

With the Stub, we can arrange the system under test's inputs and act on it by calling the checkout() method:

```
func testWhenPaymentFailsUpdatesPropertyToShowErrorAlert() {
    let viewModel = OrderDetail.ViewModel(
        orderController: OrderController(),
        paymentProcessor: PaymentProcessingStub(returning:
        .failure(TestError(id: 123)))
    )

    viewModel.checkout()

    // Assert the result: ???
}
```

How can we verify that the @Published property holding the ViewModel has changed to the value we expect when the payment processing fails?

The code we are working with is asynchronous, but it doesn't have a callback or a `Publisher` to which we can attach a handler to fulfill an `XCTestExpectation` like we did when testing the networking behavior in Chapter 10.

One easy option would be removing the artificial delay from the Stub to make the test synchronous.

I want to take this occasion, though, to show you another approach to testing asynchronous code.

How to Test Asynchronous Code When There Is No Callback

XCTest offers an asynchronous expectation that uses a given predicate to verify its fulfillment: `XCTNSPredicateExpectation`. We can use it when we cannot explicitly fulfill an expectation because the async code under test has no callback:

```swift
func testWhenPaymentFailsUpdatesPropertyToShowErrorAlert() {
    let viewModel = OrderDetail.ViewModel(
        orderController: OrderController(),
        paymentProcessor: PaymentProcessingStub(returning:
        .failure(TestError(id: 123))))
    )

    let predicate = NSPredicate { _, _ in viewModel.alertToShow
    != nil }
    let expectation = XCTNSPredicateExpectation(predicate:
    predicate, object: .none)

    viewModel.checkout()

    wait(for: [expectation], timeout: 2)
```

```
XCTAssertEqual(viewModel.alertToShow?.title, "")
XCTAssertEqual(
    viewModel.alertToShow?.message,
    "There's been an error with your order. Please contact
    a waiter."
)
XCTAssertEqual(viewModel.alertToShow?.buttonText, "Ok")
}
```

Notice how the NSPredicate only verifies that alertViewModel is not nil while the assertions on the content properties run only after the expectation fulfilled. Doing so will give us more granular failure messages than if we put all of the checks in the predicate.

Running the tests with Cmd U will show a failure with "Asynchronous wait failed: Exceeded timeout of 2 seconds, with unfulfilled expectations: ..." That's no surprise: we don't have any handling of the payment processing.

Let's subscribe to the payment processor Publisher to handle errors and make the test pass:

```
// OrderDetail.ViewModel.swift
func checkout() {
    paymentProcessor.process(order: orderController.order)
        .sink(
            receiveCompletion: { [weak self] completion in
                guard case .failure = completion else { return }
                self?.alertToShow = Alert.ViewModel(
                    title: "",
                    message: "There's been an error with your
                    order. Please contact a waiter.",
                    buttonText: "Ok"
                )
            },
```

```
        receiveValue: { _ in
        }
    )
    .store(in: &cancellables)
}
```

Now the test passes.

You might have noticed an odd timeout in the test. Why 2 seconds? In my experience, waiting for 1 second with `NSPredicate`-based expectations can sometimes result in unexpected timeouts.

Unfortunately, `XCTNSPredicateExpectation` is less performant than other asynchronous testing alternatives because it uses polling, as Apple engineer Stuart Montgomery points out in the 2018 WWDC talk *Testing Tips & Tricks*. The matchers library Nimble (see Appendix B) has a more performant way to write these expectations. If you find your code needing more than a few of these, you should consider adopting it.

When using a nonstandard timeout, extracting it in a constant will make it reusable in other tests and clarify to future readers why you chose that particular value:

```
// XCTestCase+Timeouts.swift
import XCTest

extension XCTestCase {

    /// Using a wait time of around 1 second seems to result in
    /// occasional test timeout failures when using
    /// `XCTNSPredicateExpectation`.
    var timeoutForPredicateExpectations: Double { 2.0 }
}

// OrderDetail.ViewModelTests.swift
wait(for: [expectation], timeout: timeoutForPredicateExpectations)
```

Let's move on to presenting an alert for a successful payment. We can adopt the same tactic we used for the previous test:

```swift
// OrderDetail.ViewModelTests.swift
func testWhenPaymentSucceedsUpdatesPropertyToShowConfirmation
Alert() {
    let viewModel = OrderDetail.ViewModel(
        orderController: OrderController(),
        paymentProcessor: PaymentProcessingStub(returning:
        .success(())))
    )

    let predicate = NSPredicate { _, _ in viewModel.alertToShow
    != nil }
    let expectation = XCTNSPredicateExpectation(predicate:
    predicate, object: .none)

    viewModel.checkout()

    wait(for: [expectation], timeout:
    timeoutForPredicateExpectations)

    XCTAssertEqual(viewModel.alertToShow?.title, "")
    XCTAssertEqual(
        viewModel.alertToShow?.message,
        "The payment was successful. Your food will be with you
        shortly."
    )
    XCTAssertEqual(viewModel.alertToShow?.buttonText, "Ok")
}
```

```swift
// OrderDetail.ViewModel
func checkout() {
    paymentProcessor.process(order: orderController.order)
        .sink(
            receiveCompletion: { [weak self] completion in
                guard case .failure = completion else { return }
                self?.alertToShow = Alert.ViewModel(
                    title: "",
                    message: "There's been an error with your
                    order. Please contact a waiter.",
                    buttonText: "Ok"
                )
            },
            receiveValue: { [weak self] _ in
                self?.alertToShow = Alert.ViewModel(
                    title: "",
                    message: "The payment was successful. Your
                    food will be with you shortly.",
                    buttonText: "Ok"
                )
            }
        )
        .store(in: &cancellables)
}
```

The ViewModel logic is complete. We've seen it in action through its unit tests, and we're confident it works in isolation. It's time to connect it with the view layer.

Wiring Up the View

Because the ViewModel takes care of all the conditional logic to configure and trigger the alert presentation, the only thing we have to do to present the alert in the view is connecting the ViewModel to the appropriate SwiftUI APIs:

```
// OrderDetail.swift
// ...
struct OrderDetail: View {

    @ObservedObject private(set) var viewModel: ViewModel

    var body: some View {
        VStack(alignment: .center, spacing: 8) {
            // ...
        }
        .alert(item: $viewModel.alertToShow) { alertViewModel in
            Alert(
                title: Text(alertViewModel.title),
                message: Text(alertViewModel.message),
                dismissButton: .default(Text(alertViewModel.
                buttonText))
            )
        }
    }
}
```

That's it. You can run the app to verify the integration. The HippoPaymentsProcessor in the source code for this chapter always succeeds, but if you want to verify the failure scenario, you can modify it to return an error.

Figure 13-1 shows the alerts for the success and failure scenarios.

Figure 13-1. *Alerts notifying of a successful (left) or failed (right) payment*

Alert.ViewModel does not depend on OrderDetail. If you wanted extra confidence on the whole alert presentation flow, you could extract the logic to present an alert giving a Binding<Alert.ViewModel?> value into its own View extension and write a dedicated UI test for it.

Testing the Alert Dismiss Behavior

Right now, when a user taps the alert "Ok" button, they're left with the order screen. A better UX would be to dismiss the screen as well as the alert in one go.

A pure SwiftUI way to do this would be to define a @Binding property on OrderDetail that would track the value of OrderButton's showDetail and toggle it when it's time to dismiss the screen:

```
// OrderDetail.swift
// ...
struct OrderDetail: View {
    // ...
    @Binding private(set) var isPresented: Bool
    // ...
}

// OrderButton.swift
// ...
struct OrderButton: View {
    // ...
    @State private(set) var showingDetail: Bool = false

    var body: some View {
        // ...
        .sheet(isPresented: $showingDetail) {
            OrderDetail(
                viewModel: .init(orderController: orderController)),
                isPresented: $showingDetail
            )
        }
    }
}
```

As you'll know by now, I wouldn't recommend a pure SwiftUI solution because we can't use tests to help us implement it. Adding a property to `OrderDetail` to let it know whether it's presented would also make it less reusable: it implies it should always be presented in a sheet.

There is a way to keep `OrderDetail` agnostic of its navigation and presentation hierarchy location and have part of the presentation unit testable: move as much of the logic as possible away from the pure SwiftUI components.

First, let's add a property to track the action closure to `Alert.ViewModel`:

```
import SwiftUI

extension Alert {

    struct ViewModel: Identifiable {
        // ...
        let buttonAction: (() -> Void)?
        // ...
    }
}
```

This change to the codebase is a refactor because we haven't altered the actual behavior, just the implementation. The compiler will help us identify all the files that need updating, and the tests will let us know if anything broke.

Second, let's update `OrderDetail.ViewModel` to get a closure to run when the alert dismisses:

```
// OrderDetail.ViewModel.swift
// ...
struct OrderDetail: View {

    class ViewModel: ObservableObject {
        // ...
```

```
    let onAlertDismiss: () -> Void
    // ...

    init(
        orderController: OrderController,
        onAlertDismiss: @escaping () -> Void,
        paymentProcessor: PaymentProcessing =
        HippoPaymentsProcessor.init(apiKey: "A1B2C3")
    ) {
        // ...
```

We can set {} as its value when initializing OrderDetail.ViewModel for now, just to get the code to compile:

```
// OrderButton.swift
// ...
struct OrderButton: View {
    // ...
    var body: some View {
        // ...
        .sheet(isPresented: $showingDetail) {
            OrderDetail(
                viewModel: .init(
                    orderController: orderController,
                    onAlertDismiss: {}
                )
            )
        }
        // ...
```

The next step is to verify that the generated Alert.ViewModel runs the given closure as part of its buttonAction. We can use the same approach as before: pass a Stub to simulate the success or failure behavior, wait for the payment processing to complete with a predicate expectation, and then assert that the resulting ViewModel calls the given closure:

```
// OrderDetail.ViewModelTests.swift
// ...
func testWhenPaymentSucceedsDismissingTheAlertRunsTheGiven
Closure() {
    var called = false
    let viewModel = OrderDetail.ViewModel(
        orderController: OrderController(),
        onAlertDismiss: { called = true },
        paymentProcessor: PaymentProcessingStub(returning:
        .success(()))
    )

    let predicate = NSPredicate { _, _ in viewModel.alertToShow
    != nil }
    let expectation = XCTNSPredicateExpectation(predicate:
    predicate, object: .none)

    viewModel.checkout()

    wait(for: [expectation], timeout:
    timeoutForPredicateExpectations)

    viewModel.alertToShow?.buttonAction?()
    XCTAssertTrue(called)
        // Test fails with: XCTAssertTrue failed
}
```

As usual, we wrote a dedicated test for this new behavior. Because of the XCTNSPredicateExpectation slow polling, it would be better to batch this test with the one we already wrote for the Alert.ViewModel configuration to save time. We won't do that here just to keep our examples easier to follow.

To make the test green, we need to pass the Alert.ViewModel the callback to execute:

```swift
// OrderDetail.ViewModel.swift
// ...
func checkout() {
    paymentProcessor.process(order: orderController.order)
        .sink(
            receiveCompletion: { [weak self] completion in
                guard case .failure = completion else { return }
                guard let self = self else { return }

                self.alertToShow = Alert.ViewModel(
                    title: "",
                    message: "There's been an error with your
                    order. Please contact a waiter.",
                    buttonText: "Ok",
                    buttonAction: self.onAlertDismiss
                )
            },
            receiveValue: { [weak self] _ in
                guard let self = self else { return }

                self.alertToShow = Alert.ViewModel(
                    title: "",
                    message: "The payment was successful. Your
                    food will be with you shortly.",
```

```
                buttonText: "Ok",
                buttonAction: self.onAlertDismiss
            )
        }
    )
    .store(in: &cancellables)
}
```

Finally, we need to update the SwiftUI code to make use of the action in the ViewModel:

```
// OrderDetail.swift
// ...
.alert(item: $viewModel.alertToShow) { alertViewModel in
    Alert(
        title: Text(alertViewModel.title),
        message: Text(alertViewModel.message),
        dismissButton: .default(
            Text(alertViewModel.buttonText),
            action: viewModel.buttonAction
        )
    )
}
```

I'll leave writing the test for the failure scenario as an exercise for you.

If you run the app and submit an order now, you'll see that when you dismiss the confirmation alert, the order detail sheet dismisses as well. Figure 13-2 shows this final flow.

Figure 13-2. The payment flow with production screens

Congratulations! You've now completed version 1.0.0-beta.1. Time to share it with Alberto and some of his most loyal customers for testing. I wouldn't be surprised if they came up with some final touch to implement before rolling it out officially.

SwiftUI is an excellent framework for building the view layer of our applications in a declarative way and with little effort to keep it in sync with the data it needs to display. It's immutable architecture, with views that are a function of state, not a sequence of events, helps us isolate all the presentation and behavior logic into dedicated objects that we can grow with TDD. In this chapter, we've seen such an example. We moved all the logic to generate the confirmation `Alert` and configure its callback into a dedicated ViewModel and then wrote a thin humble SwiftUI layer to consume it.

Key Takeaways

- **Whenever you require conditional logic to present a view, extract it from the SwiftUI layer**. You'll be able to use TDD to implement it, for faster feedback and better confidence.

- **You can decouple an alert configuration from SwiftUI by building a ViewModel for it.**

- **XCTNSPredicateExpectation is useful to test asynchronous code with no callbacks but has poor performance.** Consider batching multiple assertions in the same test using a predicate expectation, or adopt Nimble if you have more than a handful of those in your tests.

CHAPTER 14

Fixing Bugs and Changing Existing Code with TDD

How do you apply Test-Driven Development to change the behavior of existing code or fix a bug?

The same way as you do to write new code: by using the tests' feedback to identify the changes to make.

When updating existing behavior, you can start by editing its tests. If you have a bug to fix instead, you first write a failing test that reproduces it and then make the test pass to fix it.

Fixing Bugs Driven by Tests

The early feedback from the beta testers reported a bug in the app. After submitting an order, customers still see the checkout button, making them unsure whether their payment went through.

Let's fix this bug by flushing the order stored in `OrderController` once the payment succeeds. Where should we begin?

There is a saying in the TDD circles, *"A bug is just a test that hasn't been written yet."*

To fix a bug with TDD, you first write a failing test that reproduces it. From there, the workflow is the same as what we've been practicing so far. Follow the test failure to identify the code to write to make it pass and, as a result, fix the bug:

```
// OrderDetail.ViewModelTests.swift
// ...
func  testWhenPaymentSucceedsDismissingTheAlertResetsTheOrder() {
    // Arrange the input state with a valid order, one that
    // has items
    let orderController = OrderController()
    orderController.addToOrder(item: .fixture())

    let viewModel = OrderDetail.ViewModel(
        orderController: orderController,
        onAlertDismiss: {},
        paymentProcessor: PaymentProcessingStub(returning:
        .success(()))
    )

    // Perform the checkout and wait for it to succeed
    let predicate = NSPredicate { _, _ in viewModel.alertToShow
    != nil }
    let expectation = XCTNSPredicateExpectation(predicate:
    predicate, object: .none)

    viewModel.checkout()

    wait(for: [expectation], timeout:
    timeoutForPredicateExpectations)

    // Run the alert dismiss code
    viewModel.alertToShow?.buttonAction?()
```

```
    // Verify the order has been reset
    XCTAssertTrue(orderController.order.items.isEmpty)
}
```

If you run this test with the focused test keyboard shortcut Ctrl Cmd U, you'll see it fails.

To make the test passes and fix the bug, we need to make OrderController reset its order property as part of the alert dismiss action:

```
// OrderController.swift
// ...
func resetOrder() {
    order = Order(items: [])
}

// OrderDetail.ViewModel.swift
// ...
func checkout() {
    paymentProcessor.process(order: orderController.order)
        .sink(
            receiveCompletion: { [weak self] completion in
                // ...
            },
            receiveValue: { [weak self] _ in
                guard let self = self else { return }

                self.alertToShow = Alert.ViewModel(
                    title: "",
                    message: "The payment was successful. Your
                    food will be with you shortly.",
                    buttonText: "Ok",
```

```
                    buttonAction: {
                        self.orderController.resetOrder()
                        self.onAlertDismiss()
                    }
                )
            }
        )
        .store(in: &cancellables)
}
```

The test now passes, and the bug has been fixed. If you run the app and submit an order, you'll see the "Your Order" button shows an empty order after the order detail screen dismisses.

Changing Existing Code Driven by Tests

The early testers found the spiciness indicator unclear, so you decide to replace the chili emoji (🌶) with a fire one (🔥). How can we use the tests to drive this change in the codebase?

We already have a test for the spiciness indicator behavior. Tests are a living specification of your code's expected behavior. To change existing behavior, start by changing its tests:

```
// MenuRow.ViewModelTests.swift
// ...
func testWhenItemIsSpicyTextIsItemNameWithChiliEmoji() {
    let item = MenuItem.fixture(name: "name", spicy: true)
    let viewModel = MenuRow.ViewModel(item: item)
    XCTAssertEqual(viewModel.text, "name 🔥")
}
```

```
    // Test fails with:
    // XCTAssertEqual failed: ("name 🌶 ") is not equal to
       ("name 🔥 ")
}
```

Now that we have a failing test for the updated behavior, we can follow its lead to implement the change:

```
// MenuRow.ViewModel.swift
// ...
init(item: MenuItem) {
    text = item.spicy ? "\(item.name) 🔥 " : item.name
}
```

Run the tests, and you'll see they pass.

More often than not, developing software means editing existing code, not writing new one. These simple examples show how consistently practicing TDD will help you maintain your codebase as it matures and you shift away from a greenfield to an established codebase.

When you have a bug to fix, there will likely be an existing test you can duplicate and adapt to reproduce the incorrect behavior. If, instead, you need to modify existing behavior, then you have to look no further than its tests. Update the assertions with the new expected result and see how they fail. Existing tests give you a clear starting point to change behavior.

Having a test suite is incredibly valuable as a discovery tool when the codebase and team size grow. When you need to change an area of the code you are not familiar with, look at its tests first: they'll point you to where you'll need to go.

Key Takeaways

- **TDD helps you maintain existing code as well as write new features.**

- **To fix a bug with TDD, write a test that reproduces it, then make it pass.**

- **To update existing code, update the tests to assert the new behavior, then follow their feedback to implement it.**

CHAPTER 15

Keeping Tests Isolated with Fakes and Clear with Dummies

How can you keep tests isolated when the SUT relies on global state?

By shifting the dependency to in-memory with a Fake Test Double.

How can you make it clear which dependencies affect the behavior under test and which don't?

By using a Dummy Test Double that doesn't do anything to replace those dependencies that do not affect the behavior.

We already learned about Test Doubles, "test-specific equivalents" of the system under test dependencies, and how to use two of them. Stubs control the SUT inputs (Chapter 8 and Chapter 10), and Spies record the effects they produce on other objects (Chapter 12).

© Gio Lodi 2021
G. Lodi, *Test-Driven Development in Swift*, https://doi.org/10.1007/978-1-4842-7002-8_15

There are two more Test Doubles you might need to reach from time to time. The *Fake* replaces a dependency reproducing its behavior with a simpler implementation. The *Dummy* fills in for a dependency providing an implementation that doesn't do anything. In this chapter, we'll learn how and when to use them.

Fake: How to Bypass Slow or Stateful Dependencies

Suppose you wanted to make the order persist between app launches so that users won't risk losing it if they switch to another app and the OS kills yours. For the sake of keeping this example short, let's use `UserDefaults` as the storage layer.

Your first step is to define an abstraction for the `Order` storing capability and make `UserDefaults` conform to it:

```
// OrderStoring.swift
protocol OrderStoring {

    func getOrder() -> Order

    func updateOrder(_ order: Order)
}
```

The implementation details of how `UserDefaults` conforms to `OrderStoring` are irrelevant for what we want to explore here. You can find a working version in the source code for this chapter.

The next step is refactoring `OrderController` to use an `OrderStoring`-conforming type to read and update the order:

```
// OrderController.swift
import Combine
import Foundation
```

```swift
class OrderController: ObservableObject {

    @Published private(set) var order: Order

    private let orderStoring: OrderStoring

    init(orderStoring: OrderStoring = UserDefaults.standard) {
        self.orderStoring = orderStoring
        order = orderStoring.getOrder()
    }

    func isItemInOrder(_ item: MenuItem) -> Bool {
        return order.items.contains { $0 == item }
    }

    func addToOrder(item: MenuItem) {
        updateOrder(with: Order(items: order.items + [item]))
    }

    func removeFromOrder(item: MenuItem) {
        let items = order.items
        guard let indexToRemove = items.firstIndex(where: {
        $0.name == item.name }) else { return }

        let newItems = items.enumerated().compactMap { (index,
        element) -> MenuItem? in
            guard index == indexToRemove else { return element }
            return .none
        }

        updateOrder(with: Order(items: newItems))
    }

    func resetOrder() {
        updateOrder(with: Order(items: []))
    }
```

```
    private func updateOrder(with newOrder: Order) {
        orderStoring.updateOrder(newOrder)
        order = newOrder
    }
}
```

After this refactoring, you'd expect the tests to pass, but that's not the case. Not only do they fail but running them multiple times results in different failures.

The tests exercise the production code, which uses `UserDefaults.standard` because of the default value in the `OrderController init`.

`UserDefaults` is a storage component: it's stateful. When the tests run, they change the `UserDefaults` state by storing values in it, and those changes persist between tests and app launches.

The tests also read from `UserDefaults.standard`, meaning they depend on a stateful component and are no longer isolated. The Fake Test Double allows us to break this dependency.

We can build a Fake for `OrderStoring` that behaves like `UserDefaults` but doesn't persist its changes between individual test executions or app launches. This way, we can make the tests isolated and stateless again. Let's initialize `OrderDetail.ViewModel` with a Fake:

```
// OrderStoringFake.swift
@testable import Albertos

class OrderStoringFake: OrderStoring {

    private var order: Order = Order(items: [])

    func getOrder() -> Order {
        return order
    }
```

```swift
    func updateOrder(_ order: Order) {
        self.order = order
    }
}

// OrderDetail.ViewModelTests.swift
// ...
class OrderDetailViewModelTests: XCTestCase {

    func testWhenCheckoutButtonTappedStartsPayment
    ProcessingFlow() {
        let orderController = OrderController(orderStoring:
        OrderStoringFake())
        // ...
```

Thanks to OrderStoringFake, each test now runs with a fresh OrderStoring instance. The tests are isolated: the changes that one makes in its OrderStoringFake won't affect the others.

We could have worked around the UserDefaults statefulness by resetting its content in the setUp and tearDown methods, but doing so would have required more work and made the test case longer. Plus, we would need to replicate the setUp and tearDown harness in every test case using OrderDetail.ViewModel. Overall, using a Fake requires less code and less maintenance.

Fakes are also useful when the dependency is slow. In Chapter 10, we used a Stub to replace the unpredictable network response time with a constant 0.1-second delay and control the response it sent. Similarly, our production system might depend on slow or asynchronous computations, which we can replace with a much faster version in the tests.

Dummy: How to Provide Dependencies That Are Required but Irrelevant for the Behavior Being Tested

Objects such as ViewModels often *coordinate* different components interacting with their view. For example, `OrderDetail.ViewModel` is responsible for defining the content for the view to show, starting the payment process, and reacting to its result.

The tests for the presentation logic in `OrderDetail.ViewModel` need an instance conforming to `PaymentProcessing` to instantiate the SUT, even though the output they're testing doesn't depend on the payment outcome.

Using any of the Test Doubles we've seen so far would make the test compile but could also trick a reader into thinking the dependency is relevant for the test. A Spy would be confusing because we'd set it but never read any of its properties. Using a Fake or a Stub might suggest that the dependency provides an indirect input that affects the test outcome:

```swift
// OrderDetail.ViewModelTests.swift
func testWhenOrderIsEmptyShouldNotShowTotalAmount() {
    let viewModel = OrderDetail.ViewModel(
        orderController: OrderController(
            orderStoring: OrderStoringFake()
        ),
        paymentProcessor: ???
        onAlertDismiss: {}
    )

    XCTAssertNil(viewModel.totalText)
}
```

How can we make it clear that the `PaymentProcessing` instance doesn't affect those tests? With a Test Double that doesn't do anything – the Dummy:

```swift
// PaymentProcessingDummy.swift
```

```
@testable import Albertos
import Combine

class PaymentProcessingDummy: PaymentProcessing {
    func process(order: Order) -> AnyPublisher<Void, Error> {
        return Result<Void, Error>.success(())
            .publisher
            .eraseToAnyPublisher()
    }
}
```

Notice that this Dummy publishes a Void value in its process(order:) implementation. I defined Dummies as doubles that don't do anything, but we still need to write them so they compile. When implementing a Dummy that has to return a result, choose the simplest code you can come up with. Dummies work as placeholders only so it doesn't matter what output they provide.

Now that we built a Dummy for PaymentProcessing, we can update those tests that don't directly depend on the order payment processing to use it, for example:

```
// OrderDetail.ViewModelTests.swift
func testWhenOrderIsEmptyShouldNotShowTotalAmount() {
    let viewModel = OrderDetail.ViewModel(
        orderController: OrderController(
            orderStoring: OrderStoringFake()
        ),
        paymentProcessor: PaymentProcessingDummy(),
        onAlertDismiss: {}
    )

    XCTAssertNil(viewModel.totalText)
}
```

Dummies improve our tests "by leaving out the irrelevant code that would be necessary to build real objects and by making it clear which objects and values are not used by the SUT," as Gerard Meszaros explains in *xUnit Test Patterns*. As we discussed in Chapter 4 regarding fixtures, the easier a test is to read and reason about, the easier it will be to work with it.

We can apply the idea of a Dummy to the `onAlertDismiss` value as well, to show that it does not affect the test either:

```swift
// OrderDetail.ViewModelTests.swift
// ...
class OrderDetailViewModelTests: XCTestCase {

    let alertDismissDummy: () -> Void = {}

    // ...

    func testWhenOrderIsEmptyShouldNotShowTotalAmount() {
        let viewModel = OrderDetail.ViewModel(
            orderController: OrderController(
                orderStoring: OrderStoringFake()
            ),
            paymentProcessor: PaymentProcessingDummy(),
            onAlertDismiss: alertDismissDummy
        )

        XCTAssertNil(viewModel.totalText)
    }
}
```

Add Fakes and Dummies next to Stubs and Spies in your Test Double toolbox to write tests for any kind of behavior. Avoid depending on global state and slow computations with a Fake, and make it clear when there are components that are required but irrelevant with a Dummy.

It might not be immediately evident when you need to use a Fake or a Dummy, but that's not a problem for a developer practicing TDD. Iteration is at the core of Test-Driven Development. If using a Spy is the first thing that comes to mind to get the test to compile, go for it; you'll have time to take a step back once the test passes and see whether a different double works better.

Key Takeaways

- **Invest in keeping your test suite stateless, fast, and straightforward**. With TDD, you spend as much time in the test side of the codebase as you do in the production one; the easier it is to work within the test suite, the better.

- **The Fake Test Double replaces a dependency with a simpler version to bypass statefulness or time-consuming computations**. Use a Fake to keep your tests isolated and fast.

- **The Dummy Test Double replaces a dependency with one that doesn't do anything to make it evident it does not affect the behavior**. Use a Dummy in your tests to clarify when there are dependencies necessary for the code to build but with no input on the actual outcome being tested.

CHAPTER 16

Conclusion

Throughout this book, we used Test-Driven Development to build a fully functioning app. We moved in little steps, guided by the feedback from the tests and the compiler.

We started with a single screen showing static content and iterated our way to a dynamic ordering app, configurable from a backend, delegating payment processing to a third-party service, and persisting state on local storage.

Along the way, we learned different TDD techniques and approaches. At the base of everything is the red, green, refactor workflow: start with a failing test and make it pass in whichever way you can. It doesn't matter if the first version is ugly, suboptimal, or copy-pasted, only that the test passes. Don't be afraid of starting with hardcoded values. *Fake It, Till You Make It*. Only once the test is green, move to removing duplication and refactoring the implementation into something you are proud of.

Many times, we deployed the Partition Problem and Solve Sequentially technique to move in small iterations and shorten the feedback loop. Problems can be disassembled in smaller components that we can address one at a time in isolation. Reducing the scope of our work gives us better focus because we can hold the entire problem in our working memory. Each passing test and successful refactor is a little victory. Working your way through a test list gives you a feeling of progress and momentum.

We learned the value of making components interact through abstractions, the Dependency Inversion Principle, and how Dependency

G. Lodi, *Test-Driven Development in Swift*, https://doi.org/10.1007/978-1-4842-7002-8_16

Injection, having objects explicitly request their dependencies, results in "honest" testable code.

Applying Dependency Inversion and Injection allowed us to build Test Doubles to tackle those scenarios where the system under test wasn't a pure function.

We can use Stubs to control how dependencies affect the behavior of the system under test and Spies when it's the dependency that is affected by it. Fakes decouple our tests from the statefulness of local storage, and Dummies make it clear when a required dependency does not contribute to the test outcome.

We discovered that SwiftUI is a mighty ally to the TDD workflow. State is the single source of truth, and we cannot manipulate views directly. That means we can concentrate solely on the business logic that generates the input state and trust the framework will render it as instructed. This results in a thin and humble view layer interfacing with a presentation and behavior one that is detached from SwiftUI. We can iterate fast on both, using Xcode Previews for the former and tests for the latter.

The business logic layer has close to 100% test coverage because each line we wrote to build it was motivated by a failing test. Teams whose management imposes test coverage goals often have to go back after a feature is ready and add tests to meet the target; we got there without any extra effort.

Having extensive code coverage is terrific, but that's only the tip of the iceberg. TDD gave us benefits far more valuable.

More Than Just Testing

Once you appreciate the value of having automated tests for your code, writing unit tests first is the next obvious step. It gives you confidence and timeliness and saves you from modifying the finished production code to verify the tests.

Test-Driven Development is more than just an effective approach to writing tests for your code. In fact, its most significant benefits are not in terms of test coverage. Scores of developers have adopted TDD because they cared about testing and then stuck with it because of the design quality and productivity boost they gained.

TDD and Software Design

TDD puts a helpful pressure on how we write code, a sort of natural selection that makes only the simplest tests survive.

As we've seen throughout the book, writing code starting from its tests makes it necessary to work with small components and introduce abstractions. Doing otherwise would result in tests that are painful to work with and a slow feedback cycle. Continually ask yourself, "How can I get faster feedback?" and you'll shape your codebase in loosely coupled, highly cohesive components.

Case in point: The need to approach the UI code test-first forced us to separate the layout declaration from the logic that generates the values to populate it. As a result, we have a lean SwiftUI layer that is logic-free, and we can easily plug it into Previews. Views delegate their intelligence to their ViewModels, which represent an abstraction of the view itself and on which we have total code coverage. We could theoretically plug the ViewModels in different layouts or even use them to power a CLI application without any modification.

Using TDD also helped how we worked with dependencies outside of our control, such as the network and the third-party payment SDK. The abstractions we had to introduce to test code interacting with them had the positive side effect of making our design modular: we can replace the networking or payment component's implementation without touching the rest of the app.

Modularity also enables us to work in parallel. Once the `protocol` with the abstraction definition is in place, different team members can work on the concrete implementation and its consumers simultaneously.

You don't *need* Test-Driven Development to make good software design choices. Still, **TDD nudges you toward good design**.

The real-time feedback from the tests makes it obvious whether you are going in the right direction. If you find it's cumbersome to write a test for some code, that's a signal that the code won't be straightforward to work with in production either and it's time to take a step back and revisit the design.

TDD and Productivity

Perhaps one of the biggest causes of skepticism against Test-Driven Development is that it looks like it takes longer to write code this way. After all, you have to write the test first, then write just enough code to make it pass, and then go back and refactor it. Wouldn't it be faster to write the final implementation directly and avoid all that back and forth?

When people avoid TDD because they feel it's making them write code slower, they end up trapped in a *local maxima*. They optimize for short-term productivity at the cost of long-term effectiveness. Yes, it might be faster to write tests after the fact – or not write tests at all – but, over time, it will take longer and longer to work in a codebase built like that.

Test-Driven Development helps work nimbly even as – especially as – your codebase grows in size and complexity because of the combined effect of extensive test coverage and fine-tuned design that it produces. The test network helps you change code without fearing you'll miss a side effect and break a different area of the app. The modular and tailored design that emerged from the tests' feedback makes it easy to update, refactor, and swap implementations.

When you move one test at a time, you are never far from the stable green state. You can experiment with ease. If something doesn't work, discard the last change and you're back to safety.

The red, green, refactor workflow disassembles what may look like an untamable amount of work in bite-sized components. The end is always in sight: as soon as you make a test pass, you have something working, even though it might not be finished.

Once you bring your code to the green state, you can take a break knowing that you are leaving it in a stable place and with a clear next step – either refactor your current implementation or move to the next test in the list. When your brain knows your code works and you have a clear next step to take, it won't be wasting energy worrying about it in the background. To use productivity guru David Allen's terminology, you *close an open loop*.

Test-Driven Development helps you stay productive by keeping your codebase malleable while letting you work in small achievable and rewarding steps.

TDD and Product Development

Red, green, refactor; red, green, refactor; red, green, refactor. Test-Driven Development is an iterative process.

Working in this way and always asking yourself "Do I need this yet?" and "What's the simplest way to make this test pass?" is contagious. You'll find yourself applying Partition Problem and Solve Sequentially at a broader and broader scope.

Zoom up from writing the code for a feature to designing the feature itself, and you'll discover you can devise a simplified version to implement and ship faster. The benefit is twofold: deliver value to your customers earlier and learn about the system of work faster.

Zoom up even further, up to the product design level, and you'll begin iterating and experimenting in safe small steps, with tools like paper prototypes and A/B tests to collect data and verify assumptions before committing to expensive development phases.

Once again, TDD is not a prerequisite for this kind of product development approach. Still, **TDD makes thinking and working in small iterations a habit**. It shapes your workflow to one where gathering feedback is the most important thing.

As Spotify CEO Daniel Ek wrote in a shareholders report, "speed of iteration will trump quality of iteration."[1] Knowing how to move quickly to learn and adjust your trajectory is a winning advantage in a world changing at an ever-increasing speed.

Test-Driven Development comes with a learning curve. It might not be clear what test to write, how to shape your code's interface to inject a Test Double, or how to go from the fake implementation that made the test pass to a real one.

Don't let that stop you.

Any forward motion is better than no forward motion. Keep moving and course correct. If you don't know what test to begin with, write a test that initializes the SUT and asserts it's not nil. Once you have that test in place, try adding another assertion and see where that leads you.

Writing tests first will eventually become second nature if you consistently apply this workflow we've seen together. Like Neo seeing the Matrix's source when inside it, you'll start seeing ways to test the code you haven't written yet as soon as you read its specification.

Discovering Test-Driven Development fast-tracked my growth as a software engineer. With this book, I hope I have helped you grow too, fostering your interest for writing clean code that works and moving in small iterative steps.

The book is over, but your TDD journey has just begun. Have fun!

Endnote

1. Daniel Ek himself elaborated on this quote in a
    2020 interview on The Tim Ferriss Show podcast, at
    1:16:29.

Cheatsheet

XCTest Test Structure

Create a test case by subclassing XCTestCase and define tests as methods
with the test prefix. A good structure for your test is to separate it into
three stages: Arrange, Act, and Assert:

```swift
@testable import MyApp
import XCTest

class UserTests: XCTestCase {

    func testFullNameMergesFirstAndLastNames() {
        // Arrange the system under test and its inputs
        let user = User(firstName: "Grace", lastName: "Hopper")

        // Act on the SUT to generate the output
        let fullName = user.fullName

        // Assert the output matches the expected result
        XCTAssertEqual(fullName, "Grace Hopper")
    }
}
```

See Chapter 2 for more details.

How to Test Asynchronous Code

To test callback-based asynchronous behavior, create an
XCTestExpectation to fulfill in the callback, act on the system under test,
and make it wait for the expectation to fulfill:

```
func testAsyncSumCallsCompletionWithSum() {
    let expectation = XCTestExpectation(
        description: "Calls completion with summation result"
    )

    asyncSum(1, 2) { result in
        XCTAssertEqual(result, 3)
        expectation.fulfill()
    }

    wait(for: [expectation], timeout: 0.5)
}
```

See Chapter 2 for more details.

How to Test Asynchronous Code When There Is No Callback

Sometimes, asynchronous code doesn't use a callback-based API or a
Publisher you can subscribe to fulfill an XCTExpectation. If that's the
case, you need a different mechanism to verify whether the asynchronous
code performed the expected behavior:

```
func testAsyncSumUpdatesResultValue() {
    let summationPerformer = AsyncSummationPerformer()

    let predicate = NSPredicate { _, _ in
        return summationPerformer.result != .none
    }
```

```
let expectation = XCTNSPredicateExpectation(
    predicate: predicate, object: .none
)

summationPerformer.sum(1, 2)

// Use a "long" timeout: less than 1 second can sometimes
// result in the wait to fail.
wait(for: [expectation], timeout: 1.1)

XCTAssertEqual(summationPerformer.result, 3)
}
```

Using an XCTNSPredicateExpectation slows down your test because it relies on polling rather than a direct fulfillment mechanism. If you are dealing with code that has no callback to inject the expectation fulfillment, consider whether you can use XCTKVOExpectation or XCTNSNotificationExpectation first. If you have many of these sorts of slower tests, it's useful to introduce the open source library Nimble, see Appendix A, and use its faster .toEventually(_:) API.

See Chapter 13 for more details.

How to Test Combine Publishers

To test a Combine Publisher, define an asynchronous expectation and attach a subscriber to fulfill it if the expected behavior occurs:

```
class AsyncDivisionPerformerTests: XCTestCase {

    private var cancellables = Set<AnyCancellable>()

    func testAsyncDivisionPublishesDividedValue() {
        let divisonPerformer = AsyncDivisionPerformer()
```

```
    let expectation = XCTestExpectation(description:
    let expectation = XCTestExpectation(
        description: "Publishes divided value"
    )

    divisonPerformer.divide(dividend: 4, divisor: 2)
        .sink(
            receiveCompletion: { completion in
                guard case .finished = completion else {
                return }
                XCTFail("Expected to finish, but failed")
            },
            receiveValue: {
                XCTAssertEqual($0, 2)
                expectation.fulfill()
            }
        )
        .store(in: &cancellables)

    wait(for: [expectation], timeout: 0.1)
    }
}
```

To test the scenario in which the Publisher is expected to fail, you can change the receiveCompletion closure expectation to:

```
guard case .failure(let error) = completion else { return }
XCTFail("Expected to receive a value, failed with: \(error)")
```

You can adopt the same approach to ensure a Publisher doesn't send any value. In the receiveValue closure, use:

```
XCTFail("Expected to send no values, received \($0)")
```

See Chapter 7 for more details.

How to Test Changes to SwiftUI `@Published` Properties

To test how a `@Published` property changes over time, subscribe to its wrapped `Publisher` and test it instead. Since the `Publisher` for a `@Published` property never finishes nor fails, you can subscribe to it with the simpler `sink(receiveValue:)`. To ignore the property's initial value, use `dropFirst`:

```swift
class UserViewModelTests: XCTestCase {

    private var cancellables = Set<AnyCancellable>()

    func testPublishesUserFirstName() {
        let userFetching = UserFetchingStub(returning:
        .success(.fixture(firstName: "first name")))
        let viewModel = UserViewModel(userFetching:
        userFetching)

        let expectation = XCTestExpectation(description:
        "Eventually publishes user first name")

        viewModel
            .$userFirstName
            .dropFirst()
            .sink { firstName in
                XCTAssertEqual(firstName, "first name")
                expectation.fulfill()
            }
            .store(in: &cancellables)

        wait(for: [expectation], timeout: 0.5)
    }
}
```

See Chapter 7 for more details.

Fixture Extension

Define a static method to get a preconfigured instance of a type for testing purposes and decouple the tests from the type's init signature, and focus only on the parameters that affect the behavior under test:

```swift
// User+Fixture.swift
extension User {

    static func fixture(
        firstName: String = "first name",
        lastName: String = "last name"
    ) -> User {
        return User(firstName: firstName, lastName: lastName)
    }
}
```

See Chapter 5 for more details.

Stub Test Double

Use a Stub to control the indirect input a dependency provides the SUT:

```swift
class UserFetchingStub: UserFetching {

    private let result: Result<User, Error>

    init(returning result: Result<User, Error>) {
        self.result = result
    }

    func getUser() -> AnyPublisher<User, Error> {
        return result.publisher
            // If the behavior being doubled is asynchronous,
            // consider introducing a delay to simulate it.
```

```
        .delay(for: 0.1, scheduler: RunLoop.main).
        eraseToAnyPublisher()
    }
}
```

See Chapter 8 for more details.

Spy Test Double

Use Spy to verify the SUT's indirect output on a dependency, such as method calls or state changes:

```
class UserEventLoggingSpy: UserEventLogging {

    private(set) var loggedSignedInUser: User?

    func logUserSignedIn(_ user: User) {
        loggedSignedInUser = user
    }
}
```

See Chapter 12 for more details.

Fake Test Double

Use a Fake to replace a dependency of the SUT with a simpler version:

```
class UserStoringFake: UserStoring {

    private var user: User?

    func getUser() -> User? {
        return user
    }
```

```swift
    func setUser(_ user: User) {
        self.user = user
    }
}
```

See Chapter 15 for more details.

Dummy Test Double

Use a Dummy to provide the SUT with a value for a dependency that is necessary but irrelevant for the behavior under test:

```swift
class UserStoringDummy: UserStoring {

    func getUser() -> User? {
        return .fixture()
    }

    func setUser(_ user: User) {
        // no-op: dummies don't do anything.
    }
}
```

See Chapter 15 for more details.

APPENDIX A

Where to Go from Here

As you'll gain experience over Test-Driven Development, you'll grow hungry for more. Here are a few adjacent topics and techniques to level up your game.

Continuous Integration

How can you ensure tests pass for everyone, not only on your machine?

It's not enough for tests to pass on your computer; they need to pass on *every* computer. Moreover, when working on a team, there may be colleagues who haven't built the habit of running the tests after every change yet and inadvertently ship code that breaks other parts of the app. Or you might have an extensive test suite and want to keep a fast feedback loop by only running a subset of your tests locally.

To ensure test failures don't go unnoticed, you need a place where all the tests run every time code changes. That's the role of a *Continuous Integration* service.

Continuous Integration, CI for short, is the practice of "continuously" verifying that changes to the codebase made by different contributors can work together without breaking the software. Continuous doesn't

G. Lodi, *Test-Driven Development in Swift*, https://doi.org/10.1007/978-1-4842-7002-8

necessarily mean that tests run *all the time*; it means that they run as soon as possible. The most common setup is to run them every time a developer pushes code to the version control system shared remote repository.

There are many CI providers and flavors, but they all share the same guiding principles. You can configure them to observe your repository, check out new revisions as soon as they're received, run the tests on them, and then report the result.

A team I worked with once had a big bright LED light in the office. The light shone green by default and turned an alarming shade of red every time tests failed on CI. It was a fun way always to know if our collective work was in a stable state.

You can also use your CI to automate other useful tasks that are not related to testing, such as packaging an installable beta version of your application or even submitting the production build to App Store Connect for review.

Snapshot Testing

How can you ensure changes to a UI component don't break the screens it's used in?

User interfaces are always in flux. If you're lucky enough to work on a product that remains in business for more than a couple of years, you'll likely have to update your UI to give users something fresher and keep up to date with the latest design trends.

It's challenging to verify the effectiveness of a UI change, especially as our apps need to run on an increasing variety of screen ratios. For example, a Button view might be used in many different screens across the app; how do you ensure a change to its layout renders as expected in all of them?

This is where snapshot testing comes into play.

Snapshot testing is a methodology where the assertions are made on UI screenshots via image diffing. Every time the tests run, they generate snapshots for the UI's current state and compare them against a pregenerated baseline. If something doesn't match, they emit a failure.

Snapshot testing is particularly beneficial for automating verifications on how your UI renders edge cases, such as how labels manage long strings.

There are two popular open source libraries for snapshot testing: ios-snapshot-test-case and swift-snapshot-testing.

UI Testing

How can you ensure the app as a whole behaves as expected?

Users interact with our app from its UI, while the unit tests exercise it from the public methods of its business logic. Users see the app as a whole but unit tests look at each component in isolation.

Alongside unit tests, you can also write *UI tests* to exercise how your app's various building blocks work together.

Unlike unit tests, UI tests run in a different process than your application and can only interact with it through a proxy. This approach is called *black-box testing* – testing the app from the outside, like an impenetrable black box – and lets you write automation to simulate the actions a real user may perform and verify their outcome. There are methods to query the UI for elements matching an identifier or a search criterion and interact with them in many possible ways, like tapping, holding, dragging, swiping, and so on.

With UI testing, you can make sure the entire app flows as expected. Because it focuses only on the end behavior, it's a great tool to deploy when doing big refactors of the app's internals: if the UI tests still pass, you didn't introduce a regression.

Why not use UI testing with TDD then, if it covers end user behavior and gives us the freedom to iterate on the code?

UI testing is slower than unit testing because it has to go through the entire app's flow. It's also unfortunately flaky: it has to deal with animations, transitions, and network or database loading time.

Test-Driven Development is effective when the feedback is fast. If you were to use slow and flaky tests to drive the production code implementation, the feedback cycle would be too slow, and you'd lose all the benefits that come with TDD.

Use UI tests for those user journeys that are already stable and worth spending extra time writing – and maintaining – automated checks to ensure they won't break. The user authentication and registration, payment submission, and primary app features are all good candidates for UI testing.

When you create a new app, Xcode adds UI tests to the test action of its scheme. Because UI tests take longer to run, it's best to run them from a dedicated scheme so that they won't slow down your unit test suite.

CI is a great place to run your UI tests. You can even go as far as having a primary set of UI tests that cover the app's core features running on every build – a smoke test – and a more comprehensive but slower one that runs on a schedule – every night, perhaps.

API Integration Testing

How can you ensure your networking logic keeps working as the production API changes?

In Chapter 10, we looked at the disadvantages of making real network requests in the unit tests and how to avoid them by using fake data loaded from memory or a file.

Stubbing network requests makes the tests deterministic and fast but comes at the risk of getting out of sync with the remote API. Apps are always evolving to respond to user feedback and market demands, and so are the APIs that power them.

It can happen that the way the remote API behaves diverges from the client app expectations. Even when the API is versioned and its maintainers communicate changes ahead of time, bugs that break the compatibility can still creep in.

It's wise to put in place a set of automated tests that perform requests to the live API to ensure it returns data in the expected format. This approach is often referred to as *API integration testing*.

API integration tests necessarily hit the network and are a victim of its unreliability and relatively slow response time. As such, you should write them in a dedicated test target, so you can run the fast unit tests by themselves and keep the feedback cycle as fast as possible. Chapter 2 shows how to create new test targets.

You can configure your CI provider to run the integration tests on a schedule to ensure your app can work with the live API version.

Use Modularization to Tame Long Build Times

How do you keep the TDD feedback fast as the codebase size and build time grow?

TDD is useful only when you can get feedback from the tests fast.

As a Swift codebase grows, the build time inevitably increases with it, as the compiler has to do more work. Techniques like using a Fake Test Double help us keep tests fast, but if the app takes a long time to build, we'll still have a slow feedback cycle.

Newer, faster hardware and the Swift compiler's constant improvement may help with build time, but the bottleneck is unlikely to disappear entirely. In fact, when our hardware gives us better performances, we exploit them to write more advanced software. No one settles for a faster running version of the same old software.

An effective way to mitigate this problem, which also leaves you with a better codebase, is to invest in modularity. In a nontrivial-size project, you'll be able to identify clusters of functionality that are independent of each other. You can extract them in dedicated frameworks exposing only the user journey's entry point or functionality in the public interface.

Once you have the frameworks in place, you can split your work in two stages. First, you add or change code in the framework, enjoying faster build time because of the reduced code surface size. Once all the code is working and tidy, you can move onto the main app target, which imports the framework, to integrate the changes you made.

If you separate your components effectively, your app target will reduce to a thin coordination layer between frameworks. You'll be able to work mostly in the libraries domain, where you can get faster feedback and run through the slower full app compilation only when it's time to integrate and manually verify your changes.

Modularity improves your software design as well as your workflow. Locating independent components into different frameworks requires clear and effective boundaries and separation of concerns. You'll be able to work on each framework in isolation and parallel.

How to Convince Your Team to Adopt TDD

How can you win over TDD skeptics and adopt this workflow with your team?

Sometimes, it can be hard to convince a team to adopt Test-Driven Development.

Breaking old habits and getting used to writing tests for code that is not there yet takes time and effort. Initially, TDD gives you the feeling of moving slower; its productivity benefits become evident only after building a decent part of the software with it.

Some people push back on TDD because they got burned by it in the past. Usually, that's because they didn't have the support to learn how to write tests that didn't get in their way, resulting in a test suite that costs time instead of saving it.

Moreover, once people get comfortable with the established way of working, changing it will require effort and an initial loss of productivity; being reluctant is a natural defense mechanism.

Don't force your team into using Test-Driven Development. Instead, teach by example – be the change you want to see in the world.

Use TDD to write your code but don't make a big deal about it; don't even mention it to your teammates. People will soon begin to notice two things: your PRs always come with extensive test coverage, and working with code you wrote is straightforward because everything is in isolated and tested components.

Your colleagues will want to catch up with you and start adding tests to their code too. When it's your turn to review their code, make a point of thanking them for adding tests. Suggests improvements when necessary but always in a kind way; link articles and guides to back up your suggestions.

Eventually, people will start to come to you with questions about testing. That's the time to talk about Test-Driven Development.

Offer to pair with them to show how you work. Hold a little presentation about how you used TDD to build a useful feature in the project. Suggest it as an experiment and become your team's "TDD coach."

If a serendipitous chance to introduce Test-Driven Development doesn't come up, you can always add it to the agenda of an upcoming team meeting. Do that only after you've established a proven track record delivering great code written test-first: you need hard data to convince the skeptics.

The only way to change how a team operates is to have buy-in from each team member. Everyone is keen to adopt something new once the benefits are clear to them. By proactively showing the advantages of TDD through your work, you'll build a perfect pitch for it.

APPENDIX B

Testing with Quick and Nimble

The open source libraries Quick and Nimble offer an excellent alternative syntax to XCTest for writing tests and expectations. Quick provides an API to write tests that better expresses the behavior being tested with natural language; Nimble has a richer and more capable set of assertion methods.

Working with vanilla XCTest keeps your setup straightforward and is, therefore, easier to begin with: that's why we used it in the book. Once you mastered the fundamentals, though, you should try these libraries. If their style resonates with you, they will help you write clearer and more concise tests.

Quick and Nimble work great in pair, but it's not necessary to adopt them simultaneously. In fact, I recommend bringing Nimble in every project but suggest Quick only with teams that are already comfortable with testing.

You can find versions of the whole test suite converted to use only Nimble assertions and Quick and Nimble together in this appendix's source code.

© Gio Lodi 2021
G. Lodi, *Test-Driven Development in Swift*, https://doi.org/10.1007/978-1-4842-7002-8

Nimble

Let's start by replacing XCTest assertions with Nimble ones. Instead of

XCTAssertEqual(item.name, "a name")

we can write

expect(item.name).to(equal("a name"))

Notice how Nimble's syntax reads like a sentence: "expect item name to equal 'a name'."

There are similar alternatives for XCTAssertTrue(_:), XCTAssertFalse(_:), and XCTAssertNil(_:) with

expect(item.spicy).to(beTrue())

expect(item.spicy).to(beFalse())

expect(viewModel.totalText).to(beNil())

You can easily negate expectations by replacing to(_:) with toNot(_:):

expect(2).toNot(equal(3))

Nimble doesn't merely replace existing XCTest assertions; it offers more advanced and refined ones. For example, in our test suite we have checks on the size of array properties. With XCTest, we had to write those using equality assertions. Nimble gives us a better alternative:

expect(sections).to(beEmpty())

expect(sections).to(haveCount(3))

As discussed in Chapter 3, the most explicit assertion available helps the reader understand the test's intent. Those specialized expectations will fail with specific messages making it easier to identify the failure's cause in the tests' results, something valuable in particular on CI.

Nimble also makes testing asynchronous code more straightforward, thanks to its waitUntil(_:) and toEventually(_:) APIs.

waitUntil(_:) requires less coding than setting up and waiting for an XCTExpectation and keeps the test's flow linear:

```
waitUntil { done in
    viewModel
        .$sections
        .dropFirst()
        .sink { value in
            guard case .failure(let error) = value else {
                return fail("Expected a failing Result,
                got: \(value)")
            }

            expect(error as? TestError) == expectedError
            done()
        }
        .store(in: &self.cancellables)
}
```

The preceding example also shows Nimble's XCTFail(_:) equivalent, fail(_:), to keep the syntax homogeneous.

Nimble's option for asynchronous expectations when there is no callback to use for fulfillment is much more compact and straightforward than XCTest. Here's a comparison. With XCTest:

```
let predicate = NSPredicate { _, _ in viewModel.alertToShow
    != nil }
let expectation = XCTNSPredicateExpectation(predicate:
    predicate, object: .none)

viewModel.checkout()

wait(for: [expectation], timeout: timeoutForPredicateExpectations)
```

With Nimble:

```
viewModel.checkout()
```

```
expect(viewModel.alertToShow).toEventuallyNot(beNil())
```

Nimble's `toEventually(_:)` also has a better polling mechanism than `XCTNSPredicateExpectation`; using it won't compromise your test's speed.

Quick

If Nimble changes how you write test expectations, Quick changes how you write and organize the tests themselves. Its DSL helps you write code that better describes the behavior under test.

In Quick, the test cases are called specs, short for specifications, and individual tests are called examples to reinforce focus on *describing* instead of merely *verifying*.

Let's see how to rewrite part of the `MenuItemDetail.ViewModel` `XCTestCase` with Quick:

```
// MenuItemDetail.ViewModelSpec.swift
@testable import Albertos
import Nimble
import Quick

class MenuItemDetailViewModelSpec: QuickSpec {

    override func spec() {

        describe("MenuItemDetail.ViewModel") {

            describe("order button") {
```

```
context("when the item is in the order") {

    it("says remove from order") {
        let item = MenuItem.fixture()

        let orderController = OrderController
        (orderStoring: OrderStoringFake())
        orderController.addToOrder(item: item)
        let viewModel = MenuItemDetail.
        ViewModel(item: item, orderController:
        orderController)

        let text = viewModel.
        addOrRemoveFromOrderButtonText

        expect(text) == "Remove from order"
    }

    it("removes the item from the order") {
        let item = MenuItem.fixture()
        let orderController =
        OrderController(orderStoring:
        OrderStoringFake())
        orderController.addToOrder(item: item)
        let viewModel = MenuItemDetail.
        ViewModel(item: item, orderController:
        orderController)

        viewModel.addOrRemoveFromOrder()

        expect(orderController.order.items).
        toNot(contain
        ElementSatisfying({ $0 == item }))
    }
}
```

```
                    context("when the item is not in the order") {

                        it("says add to order") {
                            // ...
                        }

                        it("adds the item to the order") {
                            // ...

                    }

                }

            }

        }

}
```

Like Nimble, Quick helps you write tests that read like sentences: "MenuItemDetail.ViewModel, order button, when the item is in the order, says 'remove from order'."

Quick's behavior-focused syntax is a powerful aid to frame your tests based on what the code does, not how it does it. Tests that focus on behavior rather than implementation help you move faster because they do not need an update when internal implementation details change.

The difference between describe, context, and it is that you can run expectations only within an it. Use describe and context to arrange the SUT's input and it to act and assert the resulting output.

You can run code within a describe or context closure other than calling it; this allows you to Don't Repeat Yourself in the spec by extracting setup code common to a subset of tests:

```
describe("order button") {
    let item = MenuItem.fixture()
    let orderController = OrderController(orderStoring:
        OrderStoringFake())
```

```
context("when the item is in the order") {
    orderController.addToOrder(item: item)
    let viewModel = MenuItemDetail.ViewModel(item: item,
        orderController: orderController)

    it("says remove from order") {
        let text = viewModel.addOrRemoveFromOrderButtonText
        expect(text) == "Remove from order"
    }

    it("removes the item from the order") {
        viewModel.addOrRemoveFromOrder()

        expect(orderController.order.items).toNot(contain
        ElementSatisfying({ $0 == item }))
    }
}

context("when the item is not in the order") {
    let viewModel = MenuItemDetail.ViewModel(item: item,
    orderController: orderController)

    it("says add to order") {
        let text = viewModel.addOrRemoveFromOrderButtonText
        expect(text) == "Add to order"
    }

    it("adds the item to the order") {
        viewModel.addOrRemoveFromOrder()

        expect(orderController.order.items).
        to(containElementSatisfying({ $0 == item }))
    }
}
}
```

Splitting the SUT arrangement phase by leveraging `describe` and `context` is useful when there are many `its` to run with the same input state. Beware not to abuse this capability, though, or you'll end up with test code that's spread across the file and becomes hard to reason about because you cannot look at it all in the same place.

Quick is powerful and versatile, but, as Uncle Ben told young Peter Parker, *with great power come great responsibilities*: it's up to you to wield it properly. You need the awareness to gauge when your nesting of `describe` and `context` calls is going too far and the readability is suffering from it, and you need the discipline not to go down that path.

When working in a team, consider adopting Quick only once there is enough collective experience on unit testing already, and you're ready to embark on the journey of mastering this different style.

Both Quick and Nimble support Swift package manager as an installation mechanism: the adoption barrier is as low as it comes.

If you decide to adopt Quick or Nimble, don't spend time updating existing tests but only write new code with them. There's nothing *wrong* with your existing vanilla XCTest code. Unless you have slow tests, like in the case of `XCTNSPredicateExpectation`, you are better off spending time writing code that brings tangible value to your users. You'll be able to port existing tests over to use the new approach whenever you need to update them because of a change in requirements.

APPENDIX C

TDD with UIKit

The book focused on Apple's newest technologies because they are the future of Swift development. Not everyone has the luxury of working on a greenfield codebase, though, and some products need to support iOS versions older than 13 where SwiftUI and Combine are not available.

How does TDD in Swift change with UIKit? The answer is "not a lot" and, by now, that shouldn't come as a surprise to you.

Throughout the book, we often extracted logic away from the view layer and into plain classes and structs. We made SwiftUI work mainly as our business logic delivery vector: showing data to the user and reacting to their inputs. The same idea applies to UIKit development.

Keep `UIViews` and `UIViewControllers` humble; shape them into a thin glue layer between your framework-agnostic business logic and the application life cycle and user-triggered events.

In the attached source code for this appendix, you'll find a version of Alberto's app written in UIKit. Let's look at some of it to learn how to write tests for UIKit components. We'll use a finished test as the starting point to discuss techniques and design considerations.

How to Unit Test a `UIViewController`

Here's the test case for the menu item detail ViewController:

```swift
// MenuItemDetailViewControllerTests.swift
@testable import Albertos
import XCTest

class MenuItemDetailViewControllerTests: XCTestCase {

    func testConfiguresViewWithViewModel() {
        let viewModel = MenuItemDetailViewModel(
            item: MenuItem.fixture(),
            orderController: OrderController(orderStoring:
            OrderStoringFake())
        )
        let viewController = MenuItemDetailViewController(
        viewModel: viewModel)
        _ = viewController.view

        XCTAssertEqual(viewController.containerView.nameLabel.
        text, viewModel.name)
        XCTAssertEqual(viewController.containerView.priceLabel.
        text, viewModel.price)
        XCTAssertEqual(
            viewController.containerView.addOrRemoveFromOrder
            Button.title(for: .normal),
            viewModel.addOrRemoveFromOrderButtonText
        )
        XCTAssertEqual(viewController.containerView.spicyLabel.
        text, viewModel.spicy)
    }
}
```

```
func testUpdatesOrderWhenButtonActioned() {
    let item = MenuItem.fixture()
    let orderController = OrderController(orderStoring:
        OrderStoringFake())
    let viewController = MenuItemDetailViewController(
        viewModel: .init(item: item, orderController:
        orderController)
    )
    _ = viewController.view

    viewController.containerView.addOrRemoveFromOrderButton.
    sendActions(for: .touchUpInside)

    XCTAssertTrue(orderController.order.items.contains(item))

    viewController.containerView.addOrRemoveFromOrderButton.
    sendActions(for: .touchUpInside)

    XCTAssertFalse(orderController.order.items.contains(item))
}

func testUpdatesViewAfterButtonActioned() {
    let item = MenuItem.fixture()
    let orderController = OrderController(orderStoring:
        OrderStoringFake())
    let menuItemDetailVC = MenuItemDetailViewController(
        viewModel: .init(item: item, orderController:
        orderController)
    )
    _ = menuItemDetailVC.view

    let initialValue = menuItemDetailVC.containerView.
        addOrRemoveFromOrderButton.title(for: .normal)
```

```
menuItemDetailVC.containerView.addOrRemoveFromOrderButton.
sendActions(for: .touchUpInside)

XCTAssertNotEqual(
    menuItemDetailVC.containerView.
    addOrRemoveFromOrderButton.title(for: .normal),
    initialValue
)
    }
}
```

Each test accesses the view property as part of its Arrange stage:

```
_ = viewController.view
```

Accessing the view triggers internal mechanisms and results in viewDidLoad() being called. If you are using Storyboards, accessing the view also forces UIKit to decode it from its Interface Builder definition.

Speaking of Storyboards, you might have noticed that the tests instantiate MenuItemDetailViewController directly instead of loading it from a Storyboard. Avoiding Interface Builder is not a requirement for Test-Driven Development with UIKit, but it does make things cleaner because there is no way of directly injecting dependencies in a UIViewController when working with Storyboards. Instead, you need to rely on public Optional vars to set in the prepare(for:, sender:) method.

The preceding example shows another useful technique for testing in UIKit: you can simulate a user's interaction with a UIButton (and any other UIControl subclass) by calling its sendActions(for:) method:

```
viewController.containerView.button.sendActions(for:
.touchUpInside)
```

As you can see in the test, MenuItemDetailViewController uses a ViewModel. The structure of UIKit apps is based on the Model-View-Controller UI pattern, but different flavors of Model-View-ViewModel work well with it too.

Using a ViewModel, or any other technique to extract as much business and presentation logic away from the ViewController as possible, brings the same benefits we discussed when introducing the idea for SwiftUI in Chapter 6: the app core logic is free from the UI framework constraints and more straightforward to test.

Read MenuItemDetailViewController's implementation, and you'll see how little business logic it has – it truly is nothing but a glue layer:

```swift
// MenuItemDetailViewController.swift
import UIKit

class MenuItemDetailViewController: UIViewController {

    let containerView = MenuItemDetailView()

    private let viewModel: MenuItemDetailViewModel

    init(item: MenuItem, orderController: OrderController) {
        self.viewModel = .init(item: item, orderController:
        orderController)
        super.init(nibName: .none, bundle: .none)
    }

    // Override the other init methods and make them
    // `@available(*, unavailable)` to prevent consumer code
    // from instantiating the ViewController incorrectly
    // ...

    override func viewDidLoad() {
        super.viewDidLoad()
```

```
        configureViewLayout()

        containerView.configureContent(with: viewModel)

        containerView.addOrRemoveFromOrderButton.addAction(
            UIAction(
                handler: { [weak self] _ in
                    guard let self = self else { return }
                    self.viewModel.addOrRemoveFromOrder()
                    self.containerView.configureContent(with:
                    self.viewModel)
                }
            ),
            for: .primaryActionTriggered
        )
    }

    private func configureViewLayout() {
        // Set `containerView` a subview of `view` and
        // configures the Auto Layout constraints to make it
        // fill all available space.
    }
}
```

To keep the ViewController implementation minimal, you can extract the view configuration into a dedicated UIView subclass, which reads its configuration from a ViewModel. In the example, this is MenuItemDetailView.

How to Test Table Views

Most applications use some kind of list to show their data. As such, UITableViews and UICollectionViews are the bread and butter of UIKit development. I'll discuss table views in this section, but the same techniques apply to collection views.

UITableViews use a data source object to ask for the data to show and the cells to use to do it and a delegate to manage cell selection and other actions.

While it may seem natural to make the ViewController implement the UITableViewDataSource and UITableViewDelegate protocols, that only adds bloat. That logic is specialized enough to live in a dedicated object.

Here's the test for the self-contained data source for the menu list:

```swift
// MenuListTableViewDataSourceTests.swift
@testable import Albertos
import XCTest

class MenuListTableViewDataSourceTests: XCTestCase {

    func testWhenViewModelSectionsIsErrorSectionNumberIsOne() {
        let dataSource = MenuListTableViewDataSource()
        let tableView = UITableView(frame: UIScreen.main.bounds)
            dataSource.setAsDataSourceOf(tableView)

        dataSource.reload(tableView, with:
        .failure(TestError(id: 1)))

        XCTAssertEqual(tableView.numberOfSections,  1)
    }

    func testWhenViewModelSectionsIsSuccessSectionNumberIs
    NumberOfSections() {
        let dataSource = MenuListTableViewDataSource()
        let tableView = UITableView(frame: UIScreen.main.bounds)
            dataSource.setAsDataSourceOf(tableView)
```

```
        dataSource.reload(
            tableView,
            with: .success(
                [
                    .fixture(category: "a category"),
                    .fixture(category: "another category")
                ]
            )
        )

    XCTAssertEqual(tableView.numberOfSections,  2)
}

func testWhenViewModelSectionsIsErrorNumberOfRowsInSection
IsOne() {
    let dataSource = MenuListTableViewDataSource()
    let tableView = UITableView(frame: UIScreen.main.bounds)
    dataSource.setAsDataSourceOf(tableView)

    dataSource.reload(tableView, with:
    .failure(TestError(id: 1)))

    XCTAssertEqual(tableView.numberOfRows(inSection: 0), 1)
}

func testWhenViewModelSectionsIsSuccessNumberOfRows
InSectionIsSectionItemsCount() {
    let dataSource = MenuListTableViewDataSource()
    let tableView = UITableView(frame: UIScreen.main.bounds)
    dataSource.setAsDataSourceOf(tableView)

    dataSource.reload(tableView, with: .success([
    .fixture(items: [.fixture(), .fixture()])]))
```

```
    XCTAssertEqual(tableView.numberOfRows(inSection: 0), 2)
}

func testWhenViewModelSectionsIsErrorCellTextShowsError() {
    let dataSource = MenuListTableViewDataSource()
    let tableView = UITableView(frame: UIScreen.main.bounds)
        dataSource.setAsDataSourceOf(tableView)

    dataSource.reload(tableView, with:
    .failure(TestError(id: 1)))

    XCTAssertEqual(
        tableView.cellForRow(at: IndexPath(row: 0,
        section: 0))?.textLabel?.text,
        "An error occurred"
    )
}

func testWhenViewModelSectionsIsSuccessCellShowsItemName() {
    let dataSource = MenuListTableViewDataSource()
    let tableView = UITableView(frame: UIScreen.main.bounds)
        dataSource.setAsDataSourceOf(tableView)

    dataSource.reload(tableView, with: .success([
    .fixture(items: [.fixture(name: "a name")])]))

    XCTAssertEqual(
        tableView.cellForRow(at: IndexPath(row: 0,
        section: 0))?.textLabel?.text,
        "a name"
    )
}
}
```

MenuListTableViewDataSource has a reload(_:, with:) method that takes a UITableView to reload and a Result<[MenuSection], Error> to read data from.

Notice how the tests run their assertions on the table view and not on the return values from the UITableViewDataSource methods MenuListTableViewDataSource implements. By verifying the state of the table view itself, we ensure that MenuListTableViewDataSource is correctly configured as its data source.

Something else worth pointing out is how the table view uses UIScreen.main.bounds as its frame, so methods like cellFor(_:, atIndexPath:), which only returns a cell if it belongs to a visible portion of the table, will work as expected.

In the production code, MenuListViewController only needs to call the setAsDataSourceOf(_:) when configuring the table view and reload(_:, with:) when new sections come in from the API.

The same idea applies to UITableViewDelegate, as you can see in MenuListTableViewDelegate in the source code.

How to Test ViewController Navigation and Presentation

UIKit's stateful and object-oriented nature has one advantage over SwiftUI: it makes testing navigation between screens and modal presentation more straightforward.

SwiftUI views are directly coupled with their descendants in the navigation hierarchy. For example, in MenuList we had

```
// MenuList.swift
// ...
NavigationLink(destination: MenuItemDetail(/* ... */) {
    MenuRow(viewModel: .init(item: item))
}
```

At the time of writing, there is no Apple-provided solution that could make MenuList agnostic of where to navigate as a result of selecting one of its rows, even though some patterns are emerging from the community.

In UIKit, a UIViewController can easily delegate navigation and modal presentation to another object. The coordinator pattern defined by Soroush Khanlou marries well with the idea of a navigation delegate. The application coordinator (or coordinators, if your app is complex enough to be deconstructed in multiple isolated flows) can become the single component responsible for knowing how to update the navigation hierarchy.

The AppCoordinator tests show how to verify navigations and modal presentations:

```swift
// AppCoordinatorTests.swift
@testable import Albertos
import Nimble
import XCTest

class AppCoordinatorTests: XCTestCase {

    func testInitialViewControllerIsNavigationWithMenuList()
    throws {
        let navigationController = UINavigationController()
        let coordinator = makeAppCoordinator(with:
            navigationController)

        coordinator.loadFirstScreen()

        XCTAssertTrue(navigationController.viewControllers.
        first is MenuListViewController)
    }
}
```

```swift
func testPushesMenuDetailsOnNavigationStack() {
    let navigationController = UINavigationController()
    let coordinator = makeAppCoordinator(
        with: navigationController
    )
    let dummyMenuListVC = MenuListViewController    (
        menuFetching: MenuFetchingStub(
            returning: .success([])
        )
    )
    let item = MenuItem.fixture()

    coordinator.menuListViewController(
        dummyMenuListVC,
        didSelectItem: item
    )

    expect(navigationController.viewControllers.first)
        .toEventually(
            beAKindOf(MenuItemDetailViewController.self)
        )
}

func testPresentsOrderDetailOnTopOfNavigationStack() {
    let navigationController = UINavigationController()
    let coordinator = makeAppCoordinator(with:
    navigationController)

    let window = UIWindow(frame: UIScreen.main.bounds)
    window.makeKeyAndVisible()
    window.rootViewController = navigationController
```

```
expect(navigationController.presentedViewController).
to(beNil())

coordinator.presentOrderDetail()

expect(navigationController.presentedViewController)
    .toEventually(beAKindOf(UINavigationController.
    self))

let presentedNavigationController =
    navigationController.presentedViewController as?
    UINavigationController

expect(presentedNavigationController?.viewControllers.
first)
    .to(beAKindOf(OrderDetailViewController.self))
}

func testDismissesPresentedVCOnOrderCompletion() {
    let navigationController = UINavigationController()
    let coordinator = makeAppCoordinator(with:
    navigationController)

    let window = UIWindow(frame: UIScreen.main.bounds)
    window.makeKeyAndVisible()
    window.rootViewController = navigationController

    expect(navigationController.presentedViewController).
    to(beNil())

    navigationController.present(UIViewController(),
    animated: false, completion: .none)

    expect(navigationController.presentedViewController).
    toNot(beNil())
```

```
let dummyOrderDetailVC = OrderDetailViewController(
    orderController: OrderController(orderStoring:
    OrderStoringFake()),
    paymentProcessor: PaymentProcessingDummy()
)
coordinator.orderDetailViewControllerCompletedPayment
Flow(dummyOrderDetailVC)

expect(navigationController.presentedViewController).
toEventually(beNil())
    }

    private func makeAppCoordinator(with navigationController:
    UINavigationController) -> AppCoordinator {
        return AppCoordinator(
            orderController: OrderController(orderStoring:
            OrderStoringFake()),
            paymentProcessing: PaymentProcessingDummy(),
            navigationController: navigationController
        )
    }
}
```

To test that a push navigation took place, you need to account for the animated transition. The best way to do it is using Nimble's .toEventually (see Appendix B for more details):

```
expect(navigationController.viewControllers.first)
    .toEventually(beAKindOf(MenuItemDetailViewController.self))
```

Alternatively, you could inject an `animated: Bool` parameter, either in the method that results in the navigation or at the `AppCoordinator` level via its initializer. Default the parameter to `true` so that consumers in the production code don't need to worry about it and use `false` in the tests to skip the animations.

Testing modal presentation requires extra work. For the presentation to work, UIKit needs the presenter ViewController to be "on-screen." That's not the case in the tests because we instantiate `AppCoordinator` and its ViewControllers ad hoc, outside of the standard application flow. To work around that, you need to place the ViewController that will perform the presentation in a `UIWindow` and make it visible first:

```
let window = UIWindow(frame: UIScreen.main.bounds)
window.makeKeyAndVisible()
window.rootViewController = navigationController
```

What About AppKit and WatchKit?

The preceding techniques translate almost 1:1 to AppKit, the original framework for macOS app development, and WatchKit, the framework for watchOS apps.

Index

A

API integration testing, 255
AppKit, 274, *see* UIKit development
Asynchronous code
    callback process, 244, 245
    XCTestExpectation, 244

B

Bugs, 219, *see* Fixing bugs with TDD

C

Changing existing behavior, 222,
      see Changing existing code
      with TDD
Changing existing code
      with TDD, 222
    MenuRow.ViewModel, 222
Combine, 97
    Publisher, 245
    Synergy with SwiftUI, 98
Conditional view presentation
    asynchronous code, 203–207
    checkout() method, 198–203
    dismiss behavior, 210–216
    PaymentProcessing
      dependency, 201

production screens, 216
@Published properties, 200
success and failure scenarios,
    208, 209
ViewModel, 200
XCTNSPredicateExpectation, 217
Continuous Integration (CI), 251
Convenience Initializer, 73

D

Dependency Injection (DI), 89
    @EnvironmentObject
      downside approaches,
        181, 182
      MenuItemDetail, 178
      OrderController instance,
        177–180
      shared instance, 182–184
    MenuItemDetail.
      ViewModelTests, 173–175
    OrderController, 171
    shared instances, 176, 177
    TODO comments, 172
Dependency inversion
      principle (DIP)
    data fetching implementation,
      108–111

Dependency inversion
    principle (DIP) (*cont.*)
  dependency inversion vs.
    injection, 107
  fetchMenu method, 106
  inversion, 106
  MenuFetching.swift, 106
  network component, 105
  practical consequences, 107
Dummy files
  slow/stateful dependencies
    OrderStoring, 227
    UserDefaults, 228, 229
Dummy Test Double, 230, 243
  PaymentProcessingDummy, 230
Dynamic testing process
  abstraction layer, 117
  asynchronous
    expectations, 97
  cause-effect
    relationship, 115
  dependency inversion
    principle, 106–112
  ObservableObject, 99–105
  @Published properties,
    111–116

E

@EnvironmentObject, 167
  DI (*see* Dependency
    Injection (DI))
Existing code, *see* Changing
    existing code with TDD

F, G, H

Fake Test Double, 226, 248
  OrderDetail.ViewModelTests, 232
  slow/stateful dependencies
    OrderStoring, 226
  time-consuming
    computations, 233
Fixing bugs with TDD, 219
  OrderDetail.ViewModelTests, 220
Fixtures
  convenience initializer, 73
  extension, 71
  hidden cost, 70, 71
  MenuGroupingTests.swift, 72
  MenuItem code, 70
  MenuSection code, 76
  production code, 69, 77
  source code, 248
  time-saving value, 78
  type and adopting test, 76

I

Indirect inputs
  enum, 132
  MenuFetching, 130
  overview, 119
  stub test
    code configuration, 129
    error handling, 124–131
    result type, 126
    mysterious menu
      guest, 123, 124

menu fetching scenario, 120
MenuFetchingStub.swift, 122
mysterious menu guest, 123

J, K, L

JSON decoding protocol
    advantage, 142–144
    application development
        agreement, 134
    domain model, 144
    empty file option, 138
    expectations, 136
    files, 138–142
    file system and project
        targets, 140
    helper function, 141
    inline strings, 137, 138
    JSONDecoder, 136
    matching properties, 135
    MenuItem, 148
    MenuItemTests.swift, 145
    testing process, 144–148
    writing source code, 133

M

Menu ordering app, 43, 44
    Ordering flow, 168

N

NetworkFetching, 158
Network testing code

abstraction, 164
approach, 164
force-unwrapping optionals, 156
interfacing test, 156
MenuFetcher, 151, 157–160
non-deterministic tests, 151
stub test double, 160–163
third-party library, 163
unit test, 152–157
URLSession, 155, 159, 165
Nimble, 260–262

O

ObservableObject views, 99–105
    approaches, 99
    code editor, 102
    implementation's
        foundation, 100
    menuGrouping, 101
    MenuList.ViewModel.swift, 101,
        103, 104
    MenuList.ViewModelTests.swift,
        100, 105
    test navigator, 103
Optional, 18
    XCTUnwrap, 19

P

@Published properties, 240, 247
@Published property wrapper, 104
    How to test @Published
        properties updates, 111

Q

Quick and Nimble
    describe/context closure, 264
    installation mechanism, 266
    Nimble (see Nimble)
    specification (specs), 262
    XCTestCase, 262–264

R

Real world application
    data function
        categories, 47, 50
        clearest assertions, 55
        compiler, 49
        flat menu option, 48
        groupMenuByCategory(), 49
        manipulating sequences, 63
        MenuSection file, 51, 58
        naming conventions, 60–62
        production code, 62
        red/green refactor, 62, 63
        requirements, 47
        source code, 51
        strictest assertions, 52–55
        task information, 56–60
        writing code, 48
    development options, 44, 45
    MenuItem/MenuSection
        code, 65
    ordering app, 43, 44
    partition problem/solve
        sequences, 45, 46
    SwiftUI app, 65

pure functions, 67
UI code, 63–66

S

Side effects
    Hippo payments, 187
    payment flow, 185, 186
    spies, 194
    spy test double, 191–194
    third-party dependencies
        abstracting process, 189
        external objects, 189, 190
        HippoPayments
            Processor, 190
        PaymentProcessing, 190–192
    user interaction, 187
Snapshot testing, 253
Spy Test Double, 188, 192, 242
Spy testing, 249
Stub Test Double, 117, 120, 154,
    157, 160, 241
Stub testing, 248
SwiftLint, 172
SwiftUI, 63
    Synergy with Combine, 98
SwiftUI views
    @Published properties, 247
    static testing, 79
        preparatory refactor, 82, 83
        presentation logic view,
          80–82
        view implementation/
        responsibilities, 81

testability, 87, 88

ViewModel (*see* ViewModel)

T

Test combine publisher, 245, 246

Test Doubles, 121

Test-driven development (TDD)

  Arrange, Act, Assert, 31–33

  business logic layer, 236

  code clean working, 34–38

  dependency inversion and
    injection, 236

  dummy version, 28

  effective approach/writing
    tests, 237

  environmental constraints/
    natural selection, 10, 11

  fake implementation, 30–33

  isLeap function, 40

  list description, 28, 29

  manual testing, 2, 3

  Oxford English Dictionary
    defines, 1, 2

  product development,
    239, 240

  productivity, 238

  software design, 237, 238

  software developers

    automated testing, 5, 6

    dedicated function, 5

    fizz-buzz algorithm, 3

    script code, 4

    writing code, 3

software implementation, 27

strong type system, 38, 39

techniques and approaches, 235

unit tests, 6

wishful coding, 39–41

writing tests, 7–9

U

UIKit development

  AppCoordinator tests, 277

  AppKit/WatchKit, 281

  meaning, 267

  navigation hierarchy/
    presentation, 276–281

  table views, 273–276

  UIViewController, 268–272

Unit testing, 6, 254, 266

UserDefaults, 226, 228,

  see also Fake Test Double

Users interface (UI) testing,
  253, 254

V, W

ViewModel

  data-binding capabilities,
    83–85

  dependency injection, 89

  function Injection, 89, 92, 93

  implementation
    requirements, 88

  instance view, 86, 87

  MenuList, 89

ViewModel (*cont.*)
    MenuList.ViewModel
        Tests.swift, 90
    MenuSection/MenuItem, 91
    ObservableObject, 99–105
    spiciness indicator, 87

X, Y, Z

Xcode, 14
    Add a new target, 15
    Test targets, 13

XCTest
    assertions, 18
    unwrapping optionals, 18, 19
    setUp, 22
    tearDown, 22
    testing framework, 13
    wait(for:, timeout:) (*see also*
        Asynchronous code)
    XCTAssertEqual function, 17
    XCTestCase class, 16
    XCTestCase life cycle, 22–24
    XCTestExpectation, 20

Printed in the United States
by Baker & Taylor Publisher Services